MW00877374

Dan Hultquist

Understanding

REVERSE

Simplifying the New Reverse Mortgage

2021

Copyright © 2021 by Dan Hultquist

This book and it's content are protected by U.S. copyright laws.

All rights reserved. No part of this publication may be reproduced, distributed, or transmitted in any form or by any means, including photocopying, recording, or other electronic or mechanical methods, without the prior written permission of the author, except in the case of brief quotations embodied in critical reviews and certain other noncommercial uses permitted by copyright law. All artwork is the property of Visia, Inc. For permission requests, please write to the author at the address below.

For information, please contact:
Dan Hultquist
441 Greyfield Drive
Canton, GA 30115

email: dan@understandingreverse.com
website: www.understandingreverse.com

Cover design and book layout by Amy Hultquist, Visia, Inc.
Printed by Kindle Direct Publishing, An Amazon.com Company.

LEGAL DISCLAIMER

This book is presented solely for educational purposes. While best efforts have been used in preparing this book, the author makes no representations or warranties of any kind and assumes no liabilities of any kind with respect to the accuracy or completeness of the contents and specifically disclaims any implied warranties of merchantability or fitness of use for a particular purpose. Neither the author nor the publisher shall be held liable or responsible to any person or entity with respect to any loss or incidental or consequential damages caused, or alleged to have been caused, directly or indirectly, by the information or programs contained herein.

Every lending institution and borrower scenario is unique, and the strategies contained herein may not be suitable for your situation. Seek the services of a professional before obtaining any financial product or service. The information and opinions presented in this book are those of the author alone and do not represent Finance of America Reverse (FAR), nor has FAR reviewed or approved the information contained in this book.

The material contained in this book is not from HUD or FHA and this document was not approved by HUD or any government agency. Portions of federal regulations and guidelines may be highlighted in this book for clarification. However, it is recommended that the relevant regulations be read in full when needed.

"A reverse mortgage can be a useful tool in a personal financial plan for many retirees, but it is often overlooked. Much of that is due to misunderstanding. Dan Hultquist, a very knowledgeable reverse mortgage professional and trainer, understands the utility and mechanics of reverse mortgages and explains them well."

Peter H. Bell, CEO
National Reverse Mortgage Lenders Association
Washington, DC

"Baby boomer retirees need to unlock the full potential of their home equity in retirement, and reverse mortgages can be that tool. In this book, Dan Hultquist expertly breaks down the functions and internal workings of reverse mortgages in a way that can help Americans properly utilize home equity to achieve more successful retirement outcomes."

Jamie Hopkins, Director of Retirement Research
Carson Wealth Management Group
Bryn Mawr, PA

"Understanding Reverse is an indispensable tool for anyone in the reverse mortgage business or coming into the reverse mortgage industry. It is required reading for any new associate joining our law firm who will work on reverse mortgage issues."

James M. Milano, LL.M, JD, Member
Weiner Brodsky Kider PC
Washington, DC

"Understanding Reverse is the most comprehensive guide to reverse mortgages out there today. Dan Hultquist skillfully breaks down the details of this nuanced loan product to help consumers and professionals fully comprehend the benefits of the loan."

Jessica Guerin, Former Editor
HousingWire
Chicago, IL

CONTENTS

CONTENTS *(continued)*

INTRODUCTION

Loan originators and financial services professionals are encouraging the use of reverse mortgages. In many cases, this is happening even when the individual has no immediate need for one. To many that sounds like a scam. As a result, I get asked to speak to, and on behalf of, CPAs, financial planners, and banks, explaining why older homeowners are getting reverse mortgages.

Are there non-traditional uses of reverse mortgages? Do they create advantages for a much wider spectrum of homeowner? Can reverse mortgages help more than just those who are desperate and needy?

Yes, but the reverse mortgage continues to be misunderstood, resulting in some using it in the wrong ways, for the wrong reasons.

A DIFFERENT APPROACH

By now, most homeowners know that a reverse mortgage can convert home equity into cash. It can be effective in assisting those who are "house rich, but cash poor," and is commonly used to satisfy an immediate need. Many are learning it can even be used to purchase a home.

However, draws from home equity don't have to occur right away. In fact, they don't have to occur at all. There are prudent reasons for obtaining a reverse mortgage even when homeowners have no foreseeable need. In this book, we will explore those reasons.

UNDERSTANDING REVERSE

As the title of this book suggests, I felt there was a need to have a better understanding of the product. For the last 12 years, I have studied this loan program in search of the best ways to explain these concepts. You'll notice that each chapter asks a common question, and then answers it.

The primary intent of this book is to educate a broad audience on the finer details of the reverse mortgage program. Whether you are a mortgage professional, financial planner, counselor, Realtor, homeowner, or other interested party, I believe this book will help you better understand reverse mortgages.

As a matter of disclosure, I no longer originate mortgages. I am, however, a Certified Reverse Mortgage Professional (CRMP) and remain an active member of the National Reverse Mortgage Lenders Association (NRMLA).

Before you begin, please note that a **Glossary of Key Terms** and a **Principal Limit Factors Quick Reference Guide** can be found in the back of this book.

My sincere hope is that you find this book helpful and that the true power of this great program will be revealed to you.

Chapter 1

What is a REVERSE MORTGAGE?

In its most basic sense, a reverse mortgage[1] is any loan, secured by a home, where repayment is deferred to a later date — generally when the home sells.

While there are multiple types of reverse mortgages, the FHA-insured Home Equity Conversion Mortgage, or HECM, accounts for the overwhelming majority of U.S. reverse mortgages. It is the only reverse mortgage insured by the federal government, and because of their involvement, lenders can offer these loans with generous financing terms.

When I say, "federal government," I am referring to HUD, the regulator of the program, and FHA, the insurer.

- HUD: U.S. Department of Housing and Urban Development
- FHA: Federal Housing Administration, a Division of HUD

Although non-HECM products are available, the term "reverse mortgage" is often used synonymously with the government-insured HECM product.

A functional definition of a reverse mortgage is:

A federally insured loan product that allows homeowners age 62 or older to access a portion of their home equity in cash, monthly payments, or a growing line of credit.

The word "reverse" is used for two primary reasons:

1. The flow of money generally moves in reverse.
Funds on traditional mortgages move from a borrower's bank account to a lender or servicer. Reverse mortgages, however, can move funds in a lump sum, or in monthly payments, from a lender or servicer to the borrower.

Flow of Money

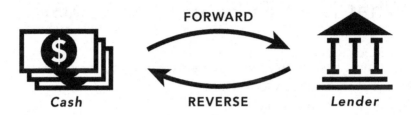

2. Loan balances tend to move in reverse.

Most traditional mortgages require principal and interest payments. This decreases the loan balance. Not requiring these payments may cause the loan balance to increase instead.

Loan Balance

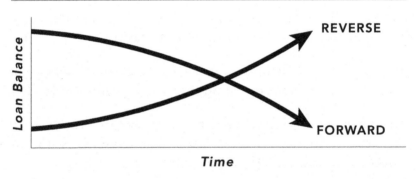

Since the flow of money generally moves in reverse and loan balances tend to move in reverse, it's obvious why it is called a reverse mortgage. However, many reverse mortgage professionals don't like the name because it implies that home equity conversion is just another mortgage product, but in reverse. In other countries, it is more aptly described as a housing pension or equity release program.

As you read this book, I think you'll find that homeowners who convert their real estate nest egg into a growing line of credit are better equipped to diversify their home equity and manage risk during retirement. As a result, reverse mortgages are more closely aligned with insurance and retirement cash flow planning.

Chapter 2

What are COMMON USES

for reverse mortgages?

Since 2013, the federally insured reverse mortgage program has gone through so many dramatic changes that it's no longer the reverse mortgage everyone imagines. As a result, many perfect candidates continue to believe that a reverse mortgage is only for a desperate homeowner with plenty of equity and no cash. But there are other advantages and common uses for the product.

I often describe three overlapping categories of homeowners who are now benefiting from a reverse mortgage.

Three Categories of Senior Homeowners

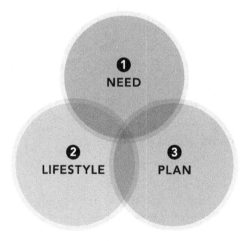

1. A reverse mortgage for immediate <u>NEED</u>[2]
These traditional HECM borrowers are house rich and cash poor. They need money now. In many cases, a reverse mortgage can help them. This might be a homeowner who can't afford medical equipment or in-home care. Payments received from a HECM can help when they, or their heirs, are unable to pay expenses.

2. A reverse mortgage to enhance <u>LIFESTYLE</u>[3]

Because reverse mortgages don't require monthly principal and interest mortgage payments, obtaining one can help with cash flow. But there are many other lifestyle advantages. Some will access the line of credit (LOC) to pay for home upgrades, travel, or even a new vehicle.

Some will receive "tenure" payments. Tenure means permanent, and these monthly payments will continue so long as the homeowner occupies the home and abides by program guidelines. This is a great way to improve the quality of life for someone on a fixed income.

3. A reverse mortgage as a financial <u>PLAN</u>

Financial planners are now recommending reverse mortgages for clients. Many of these borrowers have a disproportionate amount of their retirement savings held in real estate. Therefore, drawing part of their monthly cash flow (tax free) from their home equity nest egg will help their traditional retirement funds last longer. The primary financial planning advantage, however, is the available line of credit. This option allows homeowners to have an emergency fund that grows over time.

Regardless of which category best describes the homeowner, a reverse mortgage can give them peace of mind that they will be less likely to run out of liquid funds.

Chapter 3

When is a reverse mortgage
NOT A GOOD OPTION?

Reverse mortgage professionals find themselves touting, defending, and pitching the benefits of the HECM product because the public is still confused and largely unaware of its advantages. However, it is also important to recognize the reasons not to get one.

The fact is there are individuals for whom this is not a good fit. It would be best to identify these candidates upfront before they spend time, energy, and money to complete the mandatory counseling.

1. The home does not fit
the homeowner's long-term needs.
If the homeowner intends to sell the home soon, or if the home does not meet their long-term physical needs, a reverse mortgage may not be a good fit. While they can sell the home at any time, the program was designed to meet the needs of older Americans who wish to age in place. If the homeowner wants to stay, and is physically able to stay, they have passed my first test.

2. The reverse mortgage does
not provide a tangible benefit.[4]
The reverse mortgage needs to provide a sustainable solution throughout retirement. If the reverse mortgage offers little current or future advantage to a borrower, the homeowner should look for other options. Using a reverse mortgage to eliminate monthly mortgage payments does not always guarantee that a homeowner will have positive monthly cash flow. As a result, new regulations were implemented to ensure that monthly residual income is considered when underwriting reverse mortgages.

3. The homeowner does not adequately understand the product.

A HECM borrower or their trusted advisor must be comfortable paying property charges, maintaining the home, and managing finances. Unfortunately, some are not accustomed to these tasks. Some have competency issues that prevent them from fully understanding the loan product for which they are applying. Therefore, counseling is required to make sure all parties understand the product as well as other options available to them.

4. The homeowner wishes to protect a legacy.

Inheritance goals may, or may not, be a reason to avoid reverse mortgages. This is because homeowners who obtain a growing HECM line of credit early in retirement are better equipped to decide how future expenses are paid—by the homeowner, by the heirs, or by the home. But some homeowners wish to protect their home as a legacy for their heirs. That's a very nice gesture, and I can understand wanting to leave a "free-and-clear" home to loved ones.

Chapter 4

What are the KEY ELIGIBILITY REQUIREMENTS?

Lender guidelines vary slightly. However, key eligibility requirements remain the same: The youngest borrower must be at least 62 and they must own and occupy the property.

AGE[5]

The most important eligibility requirement may be that the borrower is age **62 or older.** Some lenders will not begin the application process until the youngest borrower is at least 62. But age is only counted in whole years. Therefore, a 69-year-old borrower who will turn 70 within six months of closing is considered 70. The advantage here is that older borrowers will generally qualify for higher principal limits. However, that does not help a borrower age 61.5. Borrowers don't become eligible to complete the loan process until they officially turn 62.

HOME OWNERSHIP

To qualify for a traditional HECM, one must not only be the homeowner but also have significant home equity. That is generally true. However, some homeowners with less equity in their homes can still qualify for traditional HECMs. They are simply "short to close," meaning that they will be required to bring funds to closing. With the HECM for Purchase program, a borrower will become a homeowner on the new property, and will be generating equity in the home by bringing funds to closing. This is often not a problem for an older adult who has just sold a property, probated the will of a parent, or liquidated an investment.

RESIDENCY[6]

The home must be the homeowner's **principal residence,** which is defined by HUD as the place where a homeowner typically spends the majority of the year. This program is not available for second homes or investment properties. Of course, this is something the lender will verify at origination. However, the HECM program also requires an annual certification confirming that the homeowner still resides in the home.

PROPERTY TYPE

These guidelines may vary slightly from lender to lender, but the following list is generally accepted for eligible property types:

- Single-family residences
- Two to four unit properties, so long as the borrower occupies one unit
- Townhomes
- Condos in a HUD-approved condominium project
- Condo units that qualify for single-unit approval (SUA)
- Planned unit developments (PUDs)
- Modular homes
- Manufactured homes that meet FHA requirements

Chapter 5

What are

MANDATORY OBLIGATIONS?

Mandatory obligations are items that will be paid, or paid off, either at closing or during the first year of the loan. These generally include mortgages against the property, closing costs, and initial mortgage insurance premiums. However, the list also includes liens and judgments that affect the owner's title, federal debt, set-asides for repairs, and funds set aside to pay property taxes or insurance due within the first 12 months.[7]

Most borrowers finance these mandatory obligations into the loan. As a result, the homeowner generally does not "pay" them until the home sells. However, mandatory obligations are very important in determining how much is money left to draw. One way to describe this is shown here:

Principal Limit – Mandatory Obligations
= Net Principal Limit

As you can see, the amount of principal that remains, after all mandatory obligations are accounted for, is referred to as the "net principal limit."

In past years, reverse mortgage borrowers commonly took 100% of their net principal limit at the time the loan closed. As a result, many such borrowers were drawing funds they didn't necessarily need. These were also considered riskier loans because the borrower had drawn all their available funds, leaving no reserve for emergencies. Because of the increased risks to both the home-owner and FHA, HUD set initial disbursement limits in 2013.

In the following example, the borrower needed to use 2/3 of their principal limit up-front to pay mandatory obligations. That does not mean the borrower has immediate access to the remaining 1/3 right away. In the next chapter we'll discuss initial disbursement limits.

Principal Limit	**$300,000**
– Mandatory Obligations	**- $200,000**
= Net Principal Limit	**= $100,000**

Chapter 6

What are

INITIAL DISBURSEMENT LIMITS?

Some summarize initial disbursement limits as "no, you can't have all your money now." But there is more to initial disbursement limits than that. Let's discuss the problem that created the need for these regulations.

From 2009 until 2013, most reverse mortgage borrowers chose the fixed-rate product. However, fixed-rate loans are closed-end loans, and borrowers received all their principal limit at closing, whether they needed it or not. Unfortunately, some borrowers spent the money and had no reserves for emergencies. This caused a wave of "technical defaults" on reverse mortgages when property charges were left unpaid. Regulators now want to know how much a borrower really needs to close their loan.

Thus, reverse mortgage borrowers are restricted to the greater of:

60% of their principal limit or
mandatory obligations + 10% of their principal limit

This is called the "initial disbursement limit" (IDL), and its purpose is to identify—and limit—the amount of funds available to the homeowner. However, the way this limit is treated will depend on the rate structure of the loan—fixed or adjustable.

Fixed-rate HECMs are closed-end loans, meaning funds (up to the IDL) may only be drawn one time at closing. There is no open line for the remaining funds.[8]

Adjustable-rate HECMs are open-end loans, meaning the remaining principal limit (plus growth) may be available to the borrower after the first year.[9]

In other words, a borrower with low mandatory obligations and a principal limit of $200,000 may be restricted to $120,000 (60%) with a fixed-rate HECM. With an adjustable-rate HECM, the same borrower would have access to $120,000 in the first year, but could also establish a line of credit for the remaining $80,000 that would be accessible after the first year.

So, can a borrower utilize 100% of their calculated principal limit at closing? Absolutely, if their mandatory obligations are high enough.

Chapter 7

What is
LIEN SEASONING?

A mortgage is a lien, or security interest, against a home. HUD has placed restrictions on the types of liens that can be paid off (using HECM proceeds) at the time of closing. In essence, certain debts must be established for one year before obtaining a HECM. This is called "seasoning."

This means that a homeowner who recently received cash by refinancing their home may have to wait for their reverse mortgage—at least until the seasoning period is over. Because the seasoning requirement is somewhat misunderstood, let's look at some key guidelines:

SEASONING FOR EXISTING NON-HECM LIENS [10]

HUD established seasoning guidelines stating that borrowers could only pay off existing non-HECM liens using HECM proceeds if the liens had been in place for at least 12 months or resulted in less than $500 in cash to the borrower.

This $500 rule is the first exception and applies to cash received at closing as well as cumulative draws.

The seasoning requirement was subsequently altered to include the closing date, not the date of application. This allows HECM loan applications to begin before the liens have been fully seasoned.

THE HELOC EXCEPTION [11]

HUD created a second exception to the rule, allowing a payoff at closing of a home equity line of credit (HELOC) that does not meet the seasoning requirements, so long as the draw from HECM funds does not exceed the borrower's calculated "initial disbursement limit."

This means that many borrowers with low mandatory obligations can now access up to 60% of their principal limit in the first year to pay mandatory obligations as well as unseasoned HELOCs.

For example, if a borrower's calculated principal limit is $200,000, then it would be fine to pay off an unseasoned HELOC (combined with closing costs) up to $120,000 (60%).

Keep in mind, this HELOC exception only applies to HELOCs and not to any other lien types. In this example, a HELOC of $50,000 wouldn't require seasoning. However, a recent $50,000 fixed-rate mortgage that resulted in cash to the borrower would require a waiting period.

CONSTRUCTION, PURCHASE, AND HECM LIENS
I often get asked if lien seasoning will disrupt the payoff of construction loans and recent home purchases. Fortunately, most of these liens are not subject to seasoning requirements because no more than $500 was given to the borrower. However, if the last distribution is given directly to the borrower for "extras," this could present an issue without proper documentation.

Regarding the payoff of HECM liens, HUD's recent regulatory changes to lien seasoning is specific only to non-HECM liens. For seasoning of HECMs, please refer to the chapter on HECM-to-HECM refinances.

Chapter 8

What is a
NON-RECOURSE LOAN?

The non-recourse feature is one of the most powerful aspects of a reverse mortgage. This feature states that the homeowner is not responsible for mortgage debt that accrues beyond the home's value. This can give the homeowner peace of mind that they will not be leaving their heirs with a bill.

The abbreviated definition of **non-recourse** is that **the home stands for the debt — not the homeowner** and not their heirs. Another succinct way of expressing this is there is **no recourse** for any mortgage loan balance other than the home.

Here is the proper definition:[12]

"FHA guarantees that neither the borrower nor their heirs will owe more than the home is worth at the time it is sold."

This should be comforting to every HECM borrower and their heirs. They can be assured that if a homeowner lives a very long time, or if property values drop or interest rates rise significantly, FHA will pay a claim to the lender so that nobody is harmed by the loan being upside down or under water.[13]

Before you say this is too good to be true, this is why FHA collects mortgage insurance premiums. FHA's Mutual Mortgage Insurance Fund (MMIF) is a pool of funds created for this purpose.

This is a primary consumer protection that makes HECMs so attractive. However, let's clarify that the loan balance technically can exceed the home's value. The lender is not ordering appraisals periodically and turning off the interest accruals.

The homeowner is simply not responsible for the amount that exceeds the home's value when the home is sold.

Non-Recourse

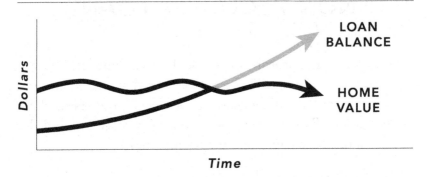

The chart above shows how the loan balance may exceed the home's value if home values do not appreciate as anticipated. In these cases, the non-recourse feature is quite advantageous. In fact, after the death of the last borrower, the property may be sold for 95% of the home's value, and again there is no recourse to the estate.

Generally, the heirs will sell the home when the last surviving borrower passes away. The reverse mortgage balance is paid off at closing just like any other lien, and the remainder would be a form of inheritance for them. However, if the home is worth less than the loan balance, the deficiency is paid through the Mutual Mortgage Insurance Fund so that the lender, borrower, and the borrower's heirs are not stuck with a bill.

Chapter 9

What maturity events
cause the LOAN TO BE DUE?

It is important to understand that at least one borrower must occupy the home as their principal residence. Therefore, the death of a borrower does not necessarily cause the HECM to end. In fact, a borrower may move out or move into assisted living, so long as one borrower still occupies the home.

However, HECM loans become due when certain events occur. These are called "maturity events" and they generally cause reverse mortgages to become due and payable.[14] Loan maturity occurs when:

- **The property is no longer the principal residence of at least one borrower.**[15] This could result from the last surviving borrower passing away, moving into assisted living, or abandoning the home.

- **The last borrower fails to occupy the property for 12 consecutive months because of mental or physical illness.** One year in assisted living is considered vacating the home.

- **A borrower does not fulfill their obligations under the terms of the loan.** Common examples would include failure to maintain the home in good condition or failure to pay property taxes, property insurance, or other property charges.

However, these maturity events do not necessarily cause the loan to become due and payable. FHA has allowed the due and payable status of a HECM to be deferred under certain conditions when a non-borrowing spouse is involved. If a non-borrowing spouse is still occupying the home, they may have additional rights under new guidelines that went into effect in August 2014. (Reference the section in this book titled, "What if a spouse is not 62 or older?" for more details on non-borrowing spouses.)

When a maturity event occurs, the borrower (or their heirs if the borrower has passed away) will need to notify the lender and declare their intentions. They then have multiple options. However, the heirs generally wish to sell or refinance the home.

Keep in mind, the borrowers and the heirs have the protection of the non-recourse feature. In fact, after the death of the last borrower, the heirs may also be able to sell the home or payoff the loan for the lesser of the mortgage loan balance or 95% of the appraised value.[16]

Note that age is also not a maturity event. While the default maturity date is commonly listed as the 150th birthday of the youngest borrower, HUD makes provisions for re-recording the security instrument if this were to ever occur.

Chapter 10

How is the
PRINCIPAL LIMIT calculated?

Principal limits provide a basis for how much the homeowner can borrow, and assuming the same data was used, principal limits should be consistent from lender to lender. To determine this figure, lenders need to know three critical numbers—age, rates, and home value.[17]

AGE

First, lenders need the age of the youngest borrower or eligible non-borrowing spouse. This is because older borrowers generally qualify for more principal. Younger borrowers—or borrowers with younger non-borrowing spouses—generally qualify for less.

RATES

Next, HECM calculators will rely on long-term interest rates. We call these "expected rates" (ER). When rates are expected to be high, HUD reduces the principal limits because loan compounding is expected to be faster through the life of the loan. Alternatively, lower expected rates produce higher principal limits.

Using these two items (age and rates) we can determine the loan's "principal limit factor" (PLF). HUD provides PLF tables to lenders. The most recent PLF tables became effective October 2, 2017.

PLFs are determined by:

- The age of the youngest borrower or eligible non-borrowing spouse
- Expected rates

For each age (up to age 99) and each expected rate between 3% and 18.875% (in 1/8% increments), HUD has provided a PLF, expressed as a percentage.

For example, a 74-year-old borrower with an expected interest rate of 5.25% would have a PLF of 47%. Below is a sample of selected ages and expected rates. (You can find a more complete schedule of PLFs in the back of the book.)

PLFs for Selected Ages and Rates

Expected Interest Rates

Age	5.00%	5.125%	5.25%	5.375%	5.50%
72	46.70%	46.00%	45.40%	44.70%	44.10%
73	47.50%	46.90%	46.20%	45.60%	44.90%
74	48.30%	47.70%	47.00%	46.40%	45.80%
75	49.20%	48.60%	47.90%	47.30%	46.70%
76	49.80%	49.20%	48.60%	47.90%	47.30%

HOME VALUE

Lastly, for calculation purposes, lenders use the lesser of the home's value or the HECM limit of $822,375. This value is also called the "maximum claim amount" (MCA), although the term itself has more to do with the lenders relationship with FHA. Nevertheless, we use the MCA for calculating principal limits.[18]

If the borrower above had a home value of $300,000, the MCA would be $300,000 and he or she would have a principal limit of $141,000, which is 47% of his or her MCA.

Chapter 11

What happens to
THE HOME after death?

There are a few misconceptions that have persisted from a time before reverse mortgages became regulated and federally insured financial tools. Correcting these fallacies has been an uphill battle.

The lender does _not_ get the home, take title to the home, or own the home or its equity in any way.

In fact, a homeowner or heir can sell the home at any time with no prepayment penalty. The HECM is simply a lien. When the home is sold, the reverse mortgage is paid off just like any other lien.

Note that we will discuss later what happens if a non-borrowing spouse is still occupying the home. However, at this moment, let's assume that is not the case.

After the death of the last surviving borrower, the heirs have multiple options. These options are easily revealed when the heirs answer these two primary questions: **"Is there equity left?"** and **"Do I want to keep the home?"**

Options for Heirs

		Is there equity left?	
		NO	**YES**
Do you want the home?	**YES**	(1.) 95% (Non-Recourse)	(2.) Payoff or Refinance
	NO	(3.) Deed-in-Lieu (Non-Recourse)	(4.) Sell the Home (Inheritance)

If the heirs want to keep the home, they can:

1. **Obtain a short payoff for 95% of the current home value.** In this way, the non-recourse feature protects the heirs' interests in a post-death transfer of the property.[19]

2. **Pay off the mortgage balance.** This generally requires the heirs to refinance the full outstanding loan balance.

If the heirs don't want the home, they can:[20]

3. **Sign a Deed-in-Lieu of Foreclosure.** If there is no economic value to selling the home, this allows the heirs to relinquish the home to the lender.

4. **Sell the home and receive a gain on the sale.** This is a very common way for borrowers to leave an inheritance to their heirs.

Clearly, the non-recourse feature is an advantage to heirs because there is no recourse for any deficiency caused by options 1 and 3. However, if the heirs wish to sell the home, they must quickly notify the servicer. They will then have six months to sell the home and HUD may approve up to two 90-day extensions.

Chapter 12

What are the

HOMEOWNER'S OBLIGATIONS?

Monthly principal and interest payments are not ongoing obligations for the homeowner. However, failure to keep up with other required homeowner obligations could cause a homeowner to default on the mortgage and may even lead to foreclosure. Let's review the obligations that must be upheld.

OCCUPY THE HOME.

Federal regulations require that a HECM borrower occupy the subject property as their "principal residence." In addition, the lender or servicer is required to document this annually with an occupancy certificate. If the home is not occupied because it is being bought using the HECM for Purchase option, the borrower has 60 days from closing to move into the home.

PAY ALL PROPERTY CHARGES.[21]

This is one of the most important messages every homeowner needs to hear. It is imperative that the homeowner always pays property charges. The only exception to this rule is when the lender sets aside a portion of the principal limit to pay certain property charges on behalf of the borrower. These property charges could include:

- Property taxes

- Homeowner insurance (hazard) premiums

- Flood insurance

- Condo association dues

- Homeowner association (HOA) dues

- Ground rent

Failing to pay these could jeopardize the homeowner's ability to stay in the home, whether they have a reverse mortgage or not.

MAINTAIN THE HOME.

This may be a little subjective, but federal regulations state the home must be kept "in good repair." As the insurer, FHA is concerned about the value of the home, so failure to maintain it can be considered a violation of the loan agreement.

Chapter 13

What is
FINANCIAL ASSESSMENT?

In 2015, the reverse mortgage program adopted a regulation called "Financial Assessment," which requires lenders to assess a borrower's credit history, property charge history, and monthly residual income. This was a dramatic change for an industry whose focus has primarily been on the value of the home. Many asked why credit matters when the loan doesn't require monthly principal and interest mortgage payments. After all, the value of the home and the age of the borrower are the primary qualifying factors.

The answer is that reverse mortgages must be a sustainable solution for each homeowner. Ideally, reverse mortgages should leave the borrower with the ability to pay their property charges and monthly bills now and in the future. The reality is HECMs may not be the proper solution for some borrowers, and the most prudent way to document sustainability is with an assessment of each borrower's financial history and status.

According to these regulations, the lender must evaluate the borrower's "willingness and capacity to timely meet his or her financial obligations and to comply with the mortgage requirements." Remember, the requirements of the loan are:

• **Keep the home in good repair.**

• **Pay property taxes.**

• **Pay homeowner insurance.**

• **Pay flood insurance if required.**

• **Pay all other applicable property charges.**

While HUD requires lenders to document a borrower's ability to meet these obligations, it is important to note that Financial Assessment does not necessarily lead to a "yes or no" answer when it comes to qualification. The results are generally used to determine if a portion of the principal limit should be set aside to ensure future obligations are met.

The lender's underwriter will complete the assessment through multiple tests that examine credit history, property charge payment history[22] and residual income.[23] If the underwriter determines that at least one test doesn't meet FHA requirements, the lender may set aside funds to pay property charges. We call this a life expectancy set-aside (LESA).

While LESAs may decrease a borrower's proceeds, they are not necessarily bad. They can provide peace of mind that critical property charges will be taken care of. In fact, many borrowers are not accustomed to paying those charges. Borrowers who are paying off existing forward mortgages have historically made those payments through an escrow account.

On one hand, fewer homeowners now qualify for reverse mortgages as a result of required financial assessment. On the other hand, those who do are better equipped to stay in their homes.

Chapter 14

What are the

INCOME REQUIREMENTS?

Many still claim the reverse mortgages do not require income, and prior to 2015 they would have been correct. That changed when HUD began requiring every lender to examine the financial capacity of the borrower and the sustainability of each HECM loan. Residual income analysis can be summarized using the following 3-step process:

1. CALCULATE EFFECTIVE MONTHLY INCOME

The underwriter will calculate monthly income, including social security benefits and employment income that is likely to continue for three years. The underwriter may also consider pension, IRA, 401(k), rental, disability, annuities, and many more sources of income or cash flow. Even assets may be counted as income. This is called imputed income or dissipation. In this context, "dissipate" means to spread the after-tax value of the asset over the youngest borrower's remaining life expectancy.

2. SUBTRACT MONTHLY EXPENSES

The underwriter will then consider monthly debt obligations from the credit report as well as a monthly calculation of property charges for all owned real estate, including but not limited to, property taxes, homeowner (hazard) insurance, and Homeowner Association (HOA) dues. The underwriter will also estimate maintenance and utility charges by multiplying the square footage of the subject property by 14 cents.

3. COMPARE THE RESIDUAL
INCOME TO HUD'S REQUIREMENTS

HUD requires that residual income be sufficient to pay for items that cannot be documented with a credit report. Those household costs tend to vary by region and family size. Therefore, the underwriter will use the following charts to determine the required threshold:

Required Residual Income by Region and Family Size

Family Size	Northeast	Midwest	South	West
1	$540	$529	$529	$589
2	$906	$866	$866	$998
3	$946	$927	$927	$1,031
4+	$1,066	$1,041	$1,041	$1,160

States by Region

Northeast	CT, MA, ME, NH, NJ, NY, PA, RI, VT
Midwest	IA, IL, IN, KS, MI, MN, MO, ND, NE, OH, SD, WI
South	AL, AR, DC, DE, FL, GA, KY, LA, MD, MS, NC, OK, PR, SC, TN, TX, VA, VI, WV
West	AK, AZ, CA, CO, HI, ID, MT, NM, OR, UT, WA, WY

If it does not appear that there is sufficient residual income, there are several compensating factors that an underwriter may consider. In addition, family size may be reduced if an underwriter wishes to document the income and credit history for a non-borrowing household member that has the financial capacity to carry their own weight.

If the residual income is still not sufficient, a portion of the principal limit may be earmarked for paying property charges using a Life Expectancy Set-Aside (LESA).

Chapter 15

What is a
LIFE EXPECTANCY SET-ASIDE?

When the underwriter determines that a borrower has failed to pass a Financial Assessment test, a LESA will generally be required. A LESA is a portion or the borrower's principal limit, set aside for paying property charges over a calculated time. There are two types:

FULLY FUNDED LESA[24]
The lender sets aside funds from the borrower's principal limit to pay three critical property charges: property taxes, homeowners insurance, and flood insurance (if needed). The lender pays these charges directly when the bills are due, like a traditional escrow account.

PARTIALLY FUNDED LESA[25]
The lender sets aside funds from the borrower's principal limit to supplement the borrower's income. The lender releases necessary funds to the borrower semi-annually to fund a small gap in residual income. The borrower is then responsible for paying critical property charges.

WHAT ARE EXTENUATING CIRCUMSTANCES AND COMPENSATING FACTORS?
Extenuating circumstances are explanations for credit imperfections (e.g., a heart attack). This will require a letter of explanation and an underwriter will determine whether the circumstance directly explains any derogatory credit.

Compensating factors are items that an underwriter will evaluate that may offset low residual income (e.g., income from a non-borrowing spouse).

HOW DO WE KNOW WHICH LESA TO USE?

Two critical questions determine the appropriate set-aside:

1. **Does the borrower have acceptable CREDIT and PROPERTY CHARGE HISTORY?**

   If **NO,** then barring any extenuating circumstances, the borrower will need a fully funded LESA.

   If **YES,** move on to Question #2.

2. **Does the borrower have acceptable monthly RESIDUAL INCOME?**

   If **NO,** then barring any compensating factors, the borrower will need a partially funded LESA.

   If **YES,** then no LESA is needed.

There are two exceptions that require a fully funded instead of a partially funded LESA.

The 75% Exception

When the projected partially funded LESA is greater than 75% of the fully funded LESA, the borrower is not eligible for the partially funded LESA. In other words, if the borrower's gap in residual income is sufficiently large, FHA would rather make sure the lender funds the property charges.

Fixed-Rate Loan Exception

Fixed-rate loans are closed-ended loans, meaning the lender cannot make future distributions to a borrower after closing, as a partially funded LESA would require. So, a fully funded LESA is required for all fixed-rate HECMs that involve a set-aside.

Chapter 16

What are the

PRODUCT OPTIONS?

The HECM can be viewed as two products: one structured as a fixed-rate mortgage, and the other structured as an adjustable-rate mortgage (ARM). Some view the HECM as one product with two rate options that have different payout guidelines.[26]

Either way, the fixed-rate HECM has rate stability, which is attractive to some borrowers. But the flexible payout options of the ARM product make it the choice for most borrowers.

HECM ARMs are tied to the movements of a published index, and rate changes will occur either annually or monthly.[27]

PRODUCT	WHEN WILL THE RATE CHANGE?
Fixed-rate HECM	The rate will not change over the life of the loan.
Monthly HECM ARM	The rate will adjust monthly.
Annual HECM ARM	The rate will adjust annually.

FIXED RATE

Fixed-rate HECM products are closed-end loans, meaning the borrower receives all their requested proceeds when the loan closes. These loans are not open for future draws. Remember, there are also disbursement limits that determine the maximum amount a borrower can receive at closing.

At closing, fixed-rate borrowers may receive the greater of the following two amounts: 60% of the borrower's principal limit, or mandatory obligations plus 10%.

Because any funds they wish to receive must be taken at the time of closing, the fixed-rate option is known as the single-disbursement, lump-sum payment option.

ADJUSTABLE RATE

Adjustable-rate HECMs are open-ended and therefore allow for multiple payout options. Ultimately, the user can achieve more with an adjustable-rate HECM, which explains the popularity of the ARM.

Open-end credit not only allows the borrower to make future draws, it also allows periodic prepayments to increase future borrowing capacity. Making such payments will reduce the loan balance and boost the borrower's line of credit for future use.

Because future draws are allowed, the initial disbursement limits can be described as follows:

Within the first year, adjustable-rate borrowers may receive the greater of the following two amounts: 60% of the borrower's principal limit, or mandatory obligations plus 10%.

ARM borrowers may access the remainder of their principal limit (plus growth) at any time after the first year, when the initial disbursement period ends.

You'll find that the most important factor when choosing between a fixed- or adjustable-rate option is not actually the rate itself. Rather, it is determining which payout option best fits the homeowner's needs.

Chapter 17

What should I know
about FIXED RATES?

Obviously, the primary difference between fixed- and adjustable-rate HECMs is that fixed-rate HECMs have rates that never change throughout the life of the loan. This stability can be very positive, especially for those with large loan balances.

However, fixed-rate HECMs only allow funds to be disbursed to the borrower once—at the time the loan funds. This is because they are closed-end loans, meaning future distributions to the borrower are prohibited. As a result, over 90% of HECM borrowers use ARM products, where they are free to request future disbursements from a growing line of credit.

DO FIXED-RATE HECMS ALLOW
FOR ANY FUTURE DISBURSEMENTS?

The answer may surprise you. It's true that fixed-rate HECMs don't have the flexibility of an adjustable-rate product. In fact, when asked this question, most reverse mortgage professionals will say no. But Jeff Birdsell, VP of professional services at ReverseVision, opened my eyes to a sensible way that fixed-rate borrowers can use undrawn funds.

The Problem

Generally, on a fixed-rate HECM, the remaining principal limit is wasted, left on the table so to speak. The borrower will never be able to use those remaining funds. They can only use 60% of their principal, right? Well, not so fast.

The Solution

The fixed-rate disbursement limit only caps what can be drawn by the borrower, not what can be paid on behalf of the borrower. It might make sense for the borrower to have funds set aside to pay property charges.[28]

Remember, this is called a life expectancy set-aside, or a LESA, which allows the lender or servicer to pay property charges on behalf of the borrower, including property taxes, homeowner insurance, and flood insurance, if needed.

Voluntary LESAs are available on both fixed and ARM products. All the homeowner needs to do is ask for one. This will set aside a portion of the remaining principal limit to be used later, on behalf of the borrower. In addition, the borrower's loan balance does not increase until a property charge is paid.

Consider a borrower who qualifies for a principal limit of $200,000. With low payoffs, the borrower may be restricted to only $120,000 (60%) of those funds. So long as the calculated LESA is $80,000 or less, the borrower can have their 60% cake and eat some of the 40% too.

Many loan originators are not aware of this trick. I believe that if this strategy were properly explained, it could result in more fixed-rate HECMs in the future.

Chapter 18

What should I know about
ADJUSTABLE RATES?

Adjustable-rate mortgages must be tied to an index that, when added to the lender margin, produces the current interest rate on the loan. When the index goes up, a borrower's interest rate goes up. Conversely, when the index goes down, a borrower's interest rate goes down.

For adjustable-rate HECMs, HUD currently authorizes the use of the Constant Maturity Treasury (CMT) index. While HUD allows the use of the 1-month CMT, lender's will generally tie their HECM ARMs to the movements of the 1-year CMT.

Keep in mind, the LIBOR was the preferred index for HECMs from the time it was authorized in 2007[29] until late 2020 when the LIBOR index was phased out for new loan originations. An example of how the interest rate is calculated is shown here:

Lender Margin	+	Index	=	Interest Rate
2.50%	+	2.00%	=	4.50%

The index is not something that can be locked. It will simply move up or down and affect the HECM's growth — the loan balance as well as the line of credit.

LENDER MARGIN
The lender has expectations about what interest they wish to receive on an ARM above the current index rate. Generally, lower margins are preferred by borrowers with high mortgage balances. However, some homeowners with a line of credit may prefer higher rates.

INTEREST RATE CAPS

Caps protect the homeowner if interest rates rise dramatically. This is critical on forward mortgages, as monthly payments can fluctuate with interest rates. Reverse mortgages don't require monthly principal and interest payments. Therefore, adjustable-rate HECM caps are there to protect the homeowner from excessive compounding of the loan balance.

The monthly HECM ARM has historically offered a 10% cap above the start rate. This means a loan that begins at 4% will never have an interest rate that exceeds 14%. This is called a "lifetime cap." Lenders have cap flexibility with the monthly adjustable product, and so you may find lifetime caps as low as 5%.

The annual HECM ARM has mandatory caps of 2% per adjustment, and 5% caps over the lifetime. This means the rate cannot rise or fall by more than 2% each year, and will not rise or fall more than 5% over the life of the loan.[30]

Chapter 19

What is the purpose
of an EXPECTED RATE?

FHA insures HECM loans, so they want to consider future rates when calculating a borrower's principal limit. We call these projections "expected average interest rates" or "expected rates" (ER) for short.

In a nutshell, expected rates estimate what rates
are expected to be in the future, and this determines
how much money the borrower may receive.

If interest rates are expected to be high, the borrower's loan balance would be expected to grow faster. This increases the risk that FHA will have to pay a claim at the end of the loan.

PLF tables provide lower principal limits when rates are expected to be high. Conversely, PLF tables provide higher principal limits when rates are expected to be low.

On a fixed-rate HECM, the expected rate is the same as the interest rate. With HECM ARMs, however, the expected rate equals the weekly average of a published index with a 10-year maturity plus the lender margin[31] as shown here:

Lender Margin	+	10-year Index	=	Expected Rate
2.50%	+	2.25%	=	4.75%

In this example, the current interest rate might be 4.50%, but the lender must use the expected rate (4.75%) when calculating principal limits. This tells FHA that the market believes rates will go up.

Keep in mind, the primary purpose of the expected rate is to determine the principal limit on a HECM loan, not to calculate interest. Therefore, the ER does not affect the compounding of the loan balance. The ER also does not affect line of credit growth.

Expected rates, however, are used for calculating a borrower's monthly payouts (tenure or term) and for setting a LESA.

10-YEAR INDEX

HECM loans are often held for 10 years or more. Therefore, we look at an index with maturity of 10 years as a way of estimating future interest rates. For HECM loans, we use the weekly average of the 10-year CMT published by the Federal Reserve. The previous week's average is generally made available on Monday afternoon. Unless Monday is a U.S. federal holiday, expected rates for new applications will change each Tuesday.

EXPECTED RATE ROUNDING

Expected rates round to the nearest 1/8th percent when calculating principal limit factors. This is true for both monthly and annually adjusted HECM ARMs. Therefore, an ER of 5.06% rounds down to 5%, while 5.07% rounds up to 5.125%.

Chapter 20

How do I LOCK my
INTEREST RATE?

With a HECM, the borrower does not lock their rate in a traditional sense. When we say "lock," we are usually not referring to a lock of the loan's interest rate, but rather the expected rate,[32] which determines the borrower's principal limit.

Remember, there are two factors that determine a borrower's principal limit: age and expected rates. While we know the borrower's age, the expected rates generally change every Tuesday. This is a concern as higher expected rates produce lower principal limits.

Without a lock, some borrowers will get less money at closing. In fact, some borrowers may not qualify if unlocked expected rates rise high enough before closing.

Imagine, in a rising interest rate environment, qualifying for less money every Tuesday until closing. A lock will solve that problem.

PRINCIPAL LIMIT PROTECTION

Expected rates are calculated each week by adding the previous week's 10-year index average to the chosen lender margin. When this figure is properly locked, the borrower's principal limit is established and protected in cases where expected rates rise between the application date and the closing date.

APPLICATION ▸ LOCK ▸ CLOSING

In addition, the borrower should receive the benefit of a "float down," where a lower expected rate at closing[33] may be used instead of the previously locked rate.

One caution is that this expected rate lock is only good for 120 days from the date the lender was assigned an FHA case number. If the closing occurs after 120 days, then current expected rates will apply.

LOCKING PROCEDURES

Lenders have slightly different guidelines regarding when, and how, a borrower's expected rate is locked. Some lenders will use a formal rate lock disclosure to verify that the borrower agrees to a lock. This will generally lock both the lender margin and the expected rate.

However, borrowers are not required to lock between application and closing; it is voluntary. But it would be counterproductive and risky not to lock, as we've already discussed.

Just remember, we are locking in expected rates to protect the principal limit. The interest rates that are tied to the interest accrual of the loan (also called the note rate) will be set by the closer at the time the loan closes. That note rate will impact interest charges, but does not determine the principal limit.

Chapter 21

What are the PAYOUT OPTIONS?

Fixed- and adjustable-rate HECMs have different payout options. As you have learned, the fixed-rate HECM is a closed-end loan and only offers a single-disbursement, lump-sum payment. But the ARM has various payout options.[34]

INITIAL DRAW

This is cash drawn at the time of closing. These funds are not available until funding, which takes place after the three-day rescission period. Nevertheless, we call this an "initial draw" because the ARM product allows for future draws.

LINE OF CREDIT (LOC)

This is the most popular payout option for multiple reasons. An open line allows a borrower to take what they need when they need it. It also allows the borrower to repay a portion of their loan balance and borrow it back in the future. The amount left in the line does not accrue interest and mortgage insurance. While this sounds a lot like a traditional line of credit on a standard mortgage, the HECM LOC provides many additional advantages we will discuss later.

TENURE PAYMENT

The word "tenure" means permanent. In this payout, the borrower's net principal limit may be converted into regular monthly draws. These payments will continue so long as a borrower occupies the home and program guidelines are followed. When explaining this option over the phone, I often call it a tenured payment or a lifetime payment. This is because many homeowners misunderstand, thinking I am explaining a 10-year plan.

TERM PAYMENT

If the calculated tenure payment is small and more funds are needed, monthly term payments may be higher, but they are not permanent. They are regular monthly draws for a specific number of months. Shorter terms provide larger payments, while longer terms provide smaller payments. After the term period ends, the reverse mortgage is still active. The borrower can still occupy the home and the loan does not have to be repaid so long as they continue to abide by program guidelines.

MODIFIED TENURE AND MODIFIED TERM

"Modified" can be defined as a combination of monthly payments and a line of credit. For example, a modified tenure is a tenure payment that also provides the client with a line of credit. The primary advantage with a modified option is the ability to combine increased cash flow with an emergency fund.

Chapter 22

Are reverse mortgages EXPENSIVE?

That's a good question and may be the toughest to answer. We simply don't have the necessary information to determine whether a loan will be expensive for the homeowner.

I often answer with "compared to what?" Can it be compared to long-term care insurance? Can it be viewed as insurance against home value declines? Can it generate retirement cash flow? The answer to these questions is yes. But it is much more than that. It is unique—there are no other financial tools like it.

Putting all of that aside for a moment, the real question behind the question is: "As a mortgage product, is it expensive?" To respond somewhat accurately, I would need to know the following:

1. **How much will the home appreciate?**
2. **How long will the homeowner have it?**
3. **How much will the homeowner draw now and in the future?**

But, wait a minute. Why does home appreciation (#1) matter? How does that impact whether the loan is expensive? If the home appreciates slowly, or not at all, or even depreciates, the non-recourse feature will protect the homeowner. When the home value is less than the loan balance, the homeowner is not responsible for the additional interest and mortgage insurance that accrues above the home's value. In other words, if the home doesn't appreciate, a HECM can be very inexpensive.

Let's move to #2. A homeowner who holds a HECM for a short period of time may find this loan to be very expensive. Imagine rolling $10,000 in closing costs into the loan balance, only to hold the loan for just one year. That can be viewed as an annual cost of $10,000 without even calculating the interest and mortgage insurance accruals. However, with the same closing costs spread over 20 years, it can be viewed as an annual cost of $500 per year. Longer terms show the mortgage to be much less expensive.

Reason #3 is important because the borrower is not required to borrow much. Some lenders require a minimum loan balance of $50 or $100 to keep the account active. The borrower may want to access significant funds later when the line of credit has grown substantially. So, are the annual costs of this loan expensive? Well, 5% interest and mortgage insurance accruals on a balance of $100 equals $5 annually. So, in this instance, not at all.

Chapter 23

What do reverse
mortgages COST?

Unlike the previous question, this answer is easy. The costs are clearly itemized at application, as lenders are required to provide a good faith estimate (GFE) of the charges. To simplify, we can break the costs into three categories: out-of-pocket, closing, and ongoing costs.

OUT-OF-POCKET COSTS

These costs generally include the appraisal fee and counseling fee. Those are two areas where the lender is required to keep their distance. As a result, the borrower will generally pay these fees directly to appraisal management companies and counseling agencies.

CLOSING COSTS

Every loan is unique, but there are generally three types of up-front costs that are rolled into the loan at closing.

1. **Origination fees:** This cannot exceed 2% of the first $200,000 in home value and 1% of the home value that exceeds $200,000, with a hard cap of $6,000.[35] The one exception is that HUD allows a minimum of $2,500.

2. **Initial mortgage insurance premiums:** This charge will be 2% of the maximum claim amount (MCA). Remember, the MCA is the lesser of the home's value or the HECM limit.

3. **Closing costs and third-party fees:** This may include settlement fees, title insurance, attorney fees, and recording fees.

These costs are sometimes off-set by lender credits or broker credits for which the homeowner may be eligible. Otherwise, HECM costs are generally financed into the loan amount so the borrower does not have to pay them out of pocket.

ONGOING COSTS

The ongoing costs of the loan depend on many factors, including: how the program is used, how much is drawn, when the funds are drawn, how much the home appreciates, and when the homeowner vacates the home.

This is a loan after all. Therefore, the amount that is borrowed will accrue interest and mortgage insurance. This will cause the loan balance to rise.

To illustrate this point, imagine a homeowner who only carries a $1,000 balance, holding the remaining amount of their principal limit in a line of credit as an emergency fund. With a 5% interest rate and 0.5% in annual mortgage insurance, the reoccurring cost to this borrower could be as little as $55 per year.

Chapter 24

Why is COUNSELING REQUIRED?

To make sure that a reverse mortgage is a good fit for the homeowner, HUD requires interested parties to undergo counseling by an independent third party. In fact, federal grant money is dedicated to counseling each year.

All borrowers, co-borrowers, and non-borrowing spouses must attend counseling, as well as guardians, conservators, and Power of Attorneys (POAs) for incompetent borrowers. Heirs are also encouraged to attend. For most homeowners, counseling may be done over the phone.

HOW DOES ONE FIND A COUNSELOR?

The loan originator should provide a list of all HUD-approved agencies that offer nationwide counseling.[36] These are called national intermediaries. The loan originator should also provide five local agencies. Otherwise, you can search online for a HECM counselor at **https://entp.hud.gov/idapp/html/hecm_agency_look.cfm** or call **800.569.4287.**

Loan originators are not allowed to steer potential borrowers to specific counselors. On the flip side, counselors are not allowed to steer potential borrowers to a particular lender, broker, or banker.

WHAT IS A BENEFITS CHECK-UP?

This is a non-profit service from the National Council on Aging (NCOA) that is designed to identify ways in which older adults can save money and cover daily expenses. During HECM counseling, the counselor may ask questions with the intention of finding federal and state resources that can improve the homeowner's ability to stay at home and meet their financial obligations.

THE PROCESS

This is a standard process for completing HECM counseling:

1. **Initial discussion:** Review the HECM product with an experienced reverse mortgage professional.

2. **Pre-counseling package:** Obtain a packet from the loan originator that includes the following documentation:

   - A list of national and local counseling agencies[37]
   - A document titled *Preparing for Your Counseling Session*
   - A comparison of various product options
   - A Total Annual Loan Cost (TALC) rate disclosure
   - An amortization schedule
   - A Use Your Home to Stay at Home booklet from the NCOA

3. **Complete counseling:** The counselor will send certificates that must be signed and dated by all parties. The lender is barred from action until a fully signed and dated counseling certificate is provided.[38] Some states also require a waiting period after counseling.

4. **Complete a loan application:** Contact your chosen loan originator to complete the application, which is called a Form 1009.

Chapter 25

What is a MORTGAGE INSURANCE PREMIUM?

HECM loans are insured by FHA and therefore a mortgage insurance premium (MIP) is required. In most cases, the borrower will roll these costs into the loan balance, and the servicer will pay these as needed on their behalf. These funds end up in the Mutual Mortgage Insurance Fund, and FHA will use it to pay out insurance claims from the lender, which can occur when the home sells for less than the loan balance.[39]

With forward mortgages, mortgage insurance exists to protect the lenders in case of defaults. With reverse mortgages, there is a similar benefit to lenders, but most homeowners and heirs are unaware that this insurance is for their benefit as well. This is how FHA pays for the non-recourse feature; the homeowner will not owe more than the home is worth at the time the house is sold.

FHA offers this insurance with no profit margin designed to benefit the federal government. In fact, changes to the program over the last few years were implemented to mitigate some of the losses to the fund.

The MIP is what allows the HECM program to offer non-recourse mortgage programs at attractive rates. If a lender were to carry the risk of a home becoming upside-down without FHA insurance, they would charge higher rates and reduce principal limits.

There are two types of insurance premiums that are charged on each loan: initial MIP and annual MIP.

INITIAL MIP (IMIP)

This fee, which is added to closing costs, is 2% of the maximum claim amount.[40] For example, a HECM for a home valued at $250,000 would require an initial premium of $5,000.

ANNUAL MIP (MIP)

The annual charges are quite different. This is calculated at an annual rate of 0.5% of the loan balance.[41] Even though this is an annual rate, it is processed monthly at a rate of 1/12th of 0.5% (approximately 0.042%).

Chapter 26

What if a SPOUSE IS NOT 62 or older?

When a spouse is not a borrower in a HECM transaction, he or she is referred to as a non-borrowing spouse (NBS). This is often due to the spouse not meeting the age requirement of 62. In a simple sense, an NBS is the spouse of a reverse mortgage borrower who will not be a borrower.

While spouses are often excluded from the reverse mortgage because they are not old enough, there can be other reasons. For example, homeowners who have prenuptial agreements, homeowners who have been remarried and want biological children to inherit their estates, or homeowners who don't intend to stay married, may all choose to leave their spouses off the loan.

THE PROBLEM

Non-borrowing spouses have historically been unprotected after the deaths of their spouses. When the borrower died, the loan became due and payable—even though the surviving spouse was still living in the home. The surviving spouse was technically not the "owner" of the home. As a result, the surviving spouse generally probated the will and then sold the home or attempted to refinance the home in his or her own name.

THE SOLUTION

Because of AARP's involvement on behalf of surviving spouses, HUD has determined that an eligible NBS should have additional rights as a homeowner. They instituted what is called a deferral period, during which the due and payable status of the loan may be deferred until a qualifying NBS dies or moves out of the home.[42] HUD also issued new PLF tables that reduce the principal limits for a borrower with an NBS.

It's important to note that under current law, the only maturity event that qualifies for the deferral period is the death of the last borrower. For example, if the borrowing spouse moves out of the home into assisted living, the NBS would not qualify for a deferral, and the loan would become due and payable.

Borrowers will still need to be at least 62 years old. However, PLFs are now based on the age of the youngest borrower or eligible NBS. This means that borrowers married to someone under 62 will have reduced PLFs.

These guidelines are applicable for loans with FHA case numbers assigned on, or after, 8/4/2014. But what about HECMs that are older than that? For those loans, HUD may offer some protection for non-borrowing spouses if the lender assigns the loan to HUD through a process known as Mortgagee Optional Election, or MOE assignment. Keep in mind, this MOE is optional for the lender.

Fortunately, non-borrowing spouses can now remain on title. While they are not borrowers on the loan, this helps to speed up the process for a MOE assignment or a deferral of the due and payable status of the loan. If you are an NBS, it may be wise to take the necessary steps to be added to title now.

Still, the guidelines for non-borrowing spouses are not that simple. We must also know which spouses are eligible for the deferral, which we'll cover next.

Chapter 27

What is an ELIGIBLE and INELIGIBLE NBS?

When HUD altered guidelines to allow spouses to continue living in their homes following the death of the borrower, it created another issue: Borrowers with an NBS could access less funds. This was because the principal limits were based on the NBS's age. This was true whether the NBS was qualified for the deferral or not.

THE CLARIFICATION

Some lenders argued that if an NBS does not qualify for the deferral, their age shouldn't be used in the calculation of the borrower's principal limit. As a result, HUD modified guidelines in 2015 to create new designations—eligible and ineligible non-borrowing spouses.[43]

An INELIGIBLE non-borrowing spouse:
- Does not occupy the home
- Is not protected by the NBS due and payable deferral provisions
- Does not have his or her age included in the calculation of the borrower's principal limit

An ELIGIBLE non-borrowing spouse:
- Occupies the home
- Is protected by the NBS due and payable deferral provision
- Has his or her age included in the calculation of the borrower's principal limit

QUALIFYING FOR THE DEFERRAL PERIOD

After the death of the last borrower, the due and payable status of the mortgage may be deferred for an eligible NBS. However, to be eligible for the deferral, the NBS must:

- Have been the borrower's spouse at the time of closing
- Have remained the borrower's spouse during the time the HECM was in service
- Have been disclosed to the lender at origination
- Have been named as an NBS in the loan documents
- Continue to occupy the home as their principal residence

If the last borrower passes away, it will be imperative that the NBS "obtain ownership of the property or other legal right to remain in the property for life" within 90 days. At that point, the NBS will need to make sure to keep up with the obligations of the HECM, including the payment of property charges, to ensure the loan does not become due and payable for other reasons.

Because an NBS only has limited protection as a homeowner and no access to the available line of credit following the death of the borrower, it is preferable not to have an NBS. However, if a spouse is under 62, the only other option is to wait.

Chapter 28

What is so special about the LINE OF CREDIT?

An amazing feature of the adjustable-rate HECM product is the line of credit (LOC). It is unique in the world of finance and is the primary reason reverse mortgages are useful in financial planning. Here are seven advantages of the line of credit:

1. Funds left in the LOC don't hurt the homeowner.

By hurt, I mean accrue interest or mortgage insurance. Those are the customary charges that would cause one's loan balance to rise. Draws from the LOC will naturally increase the loan balance, but the homeowner will only accrue charges on what they have borrowed.

2. It is OPEN-ENDED credit.

This means one can borrow from it, pay it down, and borrow from it again without restriction after the first year.[44] In fact, many will use the LOC as a form of cash flow management for business or personal use.

3. It is LIQUID home equity.

Liquid means easily converted to cash. The funds that are requested from a HECM servicer (in writing) are required to be wired to the borrower's bank account within five business days. Generally, home equity cannot be accessed so quickly. One would either need to sell the home, refinance, or obtain a home equity line of credit using traditional means to access those funds. Those methods not only take time, but also come with fees.

4. It is NOT TAXED when drawn.

Most forms of retirement cash flow are taxed. However, drawing funds from home equity is not a taxable event. Strategic draws may allow a homeowner to remain in a lower tax bracket and reduce their tax liability.

5. It is considered PLEDGED FUNDS.

The LOC is not classified as an asset. These funds are "pledged" to the borrower. This means that the growth is not taxable and that the LOC cannot be willed or given away.

6. It is SECURE.

The LOC is not capped, reduced, frozen or eliminated because of market conditions or property value declines. This enables it to be used for long-term financial planning.

7. It GROWS!

Lastly, the most compelling feature is the ability for the available LOC to grow. It grows at the same compounding rate as the loan balance, and it grows when payments are made.

Chapter 29

How does the
line of credit GROW?

The line of credit is a compelling argument as to why qualified homeowners should consider a reverse mortgage. LOC growth means these pledged funds will not only be liquid and secure, they can also grow to be much larger over time.

There are two factors that lead to LOC growth:

1. Growth rate

This causes the LOC to grow organically at a rate equal to the compounding rate.[45] This rate can be described as the current interest rate plus 0.5%. Technically, it compounds monthly at 1/12th of that rate.

Consider a loan with a lender margin of 2.5% and a current index rate of 3%. The sum of these two plus 0.5% would give the loan an LOC growth rate of 6%. In this example, even if the index were to drop to 0%, the LOC would still grow at a rate of 3%.

2. Making payments

Payments made to reduce the loan balance will also increase the line of credit. Many HECM borrowers are unaware that the LOC is boosted with each payment.[46]

The lesson to be learned is that if a borrower has cash available, it would be prudent to use it to pay down the reverse mortgage balance. They get two benefits: a lower loan balance and a larger LOC. That increased LOC will then continue to grow at the compounding rate, available for future use.

IT CAN EXCEED THE HOME'S VALUE.

The LOC may eventually exceed the home's value if the borrower holds a growing LOC for a long period of time, if a dramatic rise in interest rates make the LOC grow faster, or if property values decline. This is acceptable, and borrowers are permitted to draw funds that exceed their home's value.

PRECAUTIONS

This LOC is only available on adjustable-rate products. Fixed-rate loans are closed-end, meaning no LOC is established, and paying down the balance does not give a borrower the right to draw it back again without a refinance.

The LOC is also limited in the security deed to a maximum mortgage amount calculated at 150% of the maximum claim amount (MCA). While it is unlikely the LOC will reach that amount, HUD would require a modification of the security deed to allow draws that exceed this amount.[47]

Lastly, it is important to know that only the available LOC grows. Some borrowers use all their LOC funds and wonder why their LOC does not increase the next month. There is simply nothing to increase.

Chapter 30

What if the
home needs REPAIRS?

Renovating or repairing a home is a common reason one would consider a reverse mortgage. But there are three types of repairs:

- **Repairs that are required prior to closing**
- **Repairs for which funds are set aside to be completed after closing**
- **Renovations**

PRIOR TO CLOSING

Typical repairs that must be completed before the loan can be cleared for closing would include structural defects and health or safety concerns.[48] Structural defects could include foundation issues, electrical issues, and roof leaks. Health and safety concerns could include standing water, black mold, or even clutter that restricts proper navigation of the home.

REPAIR SET-ASIDES

For most other repairs, a portion of the principal limit may be set aside. Even if the quote is $100 for a minor repair, the lender may require a minimum set-aside amount plus an additional fee for re-inspection. Whether the quote was given by a contractor or an appraiser, estimated repairs that require a set-aside will be marked up. All such repairs are now calculated at 1.5 times (150%) the estimated amount.

RENOVATIONS

When a homeowner decides that this is the home where they wish to spend their remaining years, there are often renovations to be made that can enhance mobility. These could include handrails in the bathrooms, a walk-in bathtub, and railings or ramps near outside steps. These may be completed prior to closing, or after closing using a line of credit.

For a major overhaul or remodel, HUD has a limit of 15% of the maximum claim amount. Items that exceed this limit should be completed prior to closing.[49]

Chapter 31

What is a
HECM-TO-HECM REFINANCE?

With a HECM-to-HECM refinance (H2H refi), the borrower will be paying off an existing HECM with a new HECM. But HECM ARMs have a built-in disincentive to refinance—the borrower's net principal limit continues to grow over time. This means that homeowners who have not borrowed all their available funds have a growing line of credit that often makes refinancing unnecessary.

WHY WOULD SOMEONE REFINANCE THEIR HECM?

There are many legitimate reasons why a reverse mortgage borrower may want to refinance their existing HECM. For example:

- A homeowner may wish to have a spouse added to the reverse mortgage. With an H2H refi, the spouse would have additional protection and rights.

- Property values may have increased through appreciation or renovation. This offers the homeowner access to additional funds.

- The homeowner may wish to change loan terms, including rate structure (fixed or adjustable) and interest rate, or borrow under more favorable guidelines.

One additional reason for an H2H refi is that prior to 2008, many home values were capped by FHA county lending limits. In 2008, the Housing and Economic Recovery Act (HERA) established a nationwide lending limit. That amount has increased several times and currently stands at $822,375. For this reason, homeowners with higher-valued homes who obtained their HECM with restrictive loan limits might want access to more equity.

The National Reverse Mortgage Lenders Association (NRMLA) has issued guidance designed to discourage "loan flipping" or "churning," a practice where a loan originator repeatedly refinances an existing HECM borrower unnecessarily.

WHAT ARE NRMLA'S ADVISORIES REGARDING CHURNING?

NRMLA members are advised to wait at least 18 months to refinance a HECM. Even after 18 months, there must be a "bona fide advantage" to the consumer. This means that either the refinance will need to begin with a written request to add a family member to the loan, or the following two tests must be passed:[50]

The Closing Cost Test

The increase in principal limit must be at least five times the costs of the transaction. For example, a loan with $5,000 in closing costs must produce an increase in principal limit of at least $25,000.

The Loan Proceeds Test

The available benefit amount from the refinance must be at least 5% of the borrower's principal limit. For example, a borrower with a $200,000 new principal limit must have at least $10,000 in funds generated by the refinance. These available funds, also known as "net principal limit" may be drawn at closing, held in a line of credit, or distributed over time in the form of monthly payments.

Chapter 32

What are the basics of
HECM FINANCIAL PLANNING?

Financial planners, advisors, CPAs, tax planners, estate planners, insurance agents, and other finance professionals are realizing that obtaining a reverse mortgage early can maximize retirement assets. Much of this is a result of the growing line of credit, which can act as a reserve, a form of insurance, or an alternate source of retirement cash flow.

THE HECM ARM IS THE KEY.

When using the HECM as a financial planning tool, the fixed-rate HECM is generally not the best option. Here's why:

1. Future Draws

Fixed-rate HECMs are single-disbursement, lump-sum loans. This means that future draws are not available. Financial planning, by definition, involves creating alternatives for the future, and the HECM ARM provides many options.

2. Making Payments

When prepayments are made on the HECM Fixed, it reduces the unpaid principal balance. That's all it does. However, when prepayments are made on an adjustable-rate HECM, it not only reduces the unpaid principal balance, but also boosts the LOC.[51]

NON-TAXABLE DRAWS

Another basic financial planning advantage is that draws from the growing LOC are not taxed as income. This is not true when drawing retirement cash flow from other sources like Social Security, an IRA, or a 401(k). Armed with this alternate source of funds, financial planners may be able to control how much a client shows each year in adjusted gross income.

INSURANCE

When a homeowner uses a HECM as part of a comprehensive financial planning strategy, it can act as form of insurance against declining home values. If the value of the home declines, an established LOC will continue to grow.

LONGEVITY RISK

The biggest concern in retirement is running out of money. However, as the homeowner gets older, the LOC grows as the retirement portfolio generally declines. The HECM is a way to hedge against, or manage, longevity risk.

As you can see, the HECM is a great financial planning tool because it not only offers access to emergency funds, but also provides a growing LOC. At any time, the homeowner can convert the LOC into monthly payments for additional income, to pay for in-home care, or to shore up reserves if the retirement portfolio is depleted.

While many continue to use a reverse mortgage for cash, using it as a financial planning tool leads to greater security and future cash-flow options in retirement.

Chapter 33

Aren't reverse mortgages
for the DESPERATE?

No. But, I can understand why many believe this is true. There is a common misconception that the reverse mortgage is a "loan of last resort" for desperate homeowners facing foreclosure or bankruptcy. This stems from poor marketing that has given the public the wrong impression.

Yes, the reverse mortgage is a terrific, life-saving program for those who are house rich but cash poor and need money right now. It can be viewed as an ATM machine for homeowners with significant equity but no cash. Unfortunately, many have taken this usage to its extreme and began to use this as a full-blown cash-out refinance. This is surely one of the many uses for HECMs and can have a dramatic positive impact on a homeowner's quality of life. However, it may not be the optimal strategy for many homeowners.

Let's look at the original intent of the reverse mortgage program. HUD's Handbook 4235 was designed to provide guidance on how the program should operate, and it starts with the purpose of the program:

**"To enable elderly homeowners to convert
the equity in their homes to monthly streams
of income and/or lines of credit."**[52]

Unfortunately, some brokers and lenders are not well-equipped to explain or demonstrate the financial planning advantages this program has for those who are not desperate or who are independently wealthy. Many ideal candidates have no immediate need for government-insured funds, and the program can be a prudent option for them if used properly. Being able to recognize the alternate uses of home equity in retirement requires one to take a long-term financial-planning view. Remember, the program was not designed to be a quick fix, but rather to provide two things:

1. **A monthly stream of income, and/or**
2. **A line of credit for future use**

Of course, these two payout options may also be very useful for the desperate and needy. However, our primary objective as reverse mortgage professionals is to make sure our clients have long-term strategies for occupying their homes. They need the ability to not only pay their living expenses, but also any contingencies that may arise. The line of credit makes this possible.

Chapter 34

What are the ADVANTAGES
of MAKING PAYMENTS?

There are significant advantages to making payments toward HECM loan balances that are not well known. Many homeowners are too intrigued by the fact that HECMs don't require a payment. Unfortunately, they miss a great opportunity to maximize some of the loan's advantages.

LOAN BALANCE REDUCTION

Of course, payments reduce the homeowner's loan balance. This advantage is no different than most other loans. If the borrower can make payments, then reducing the loan balance on a reverse mortgage will reduce the interest and mortgage insurance accruals on the loan. This can protect the homeowner's equity as they will owe less on the mortgage.

A. Making Regular Payments *(Just Like Forward Mortgages)*

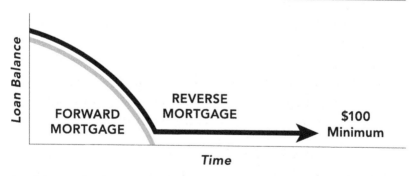

As this graph shows, the forward mortgage (in gray) is paid off completely (loan balance = $0). If the same payments are consistently applied to the reverse mortgage, the reduction in loan balance would be similar. The HECM loan balance, however, is paid down to a recommended $100 loan balance. This keeps the mortgage active and preserves the line of credit.[53] **It is not advantageous to pay off the loan completely, as this would close the HECM.**[54]

Many HECM borrowers will make periodic payments as investments mature or as they sell off other assets. This is advantageous as well.

B. Making Periodic Payments

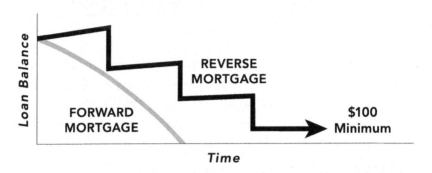

As the graph shows, interest and mortgage insurance accruals will cause the loan to rise. The payments, also known as "pre-payments" will knock the balance down. The loan balance will rise again until the next pre-payment is made.

BOOSTING THE LOC

A second advantage to making payments toward an adjustable-rate HECM loan balance is a potential boost in the LOC.[55] This opens up one of the hidden secrets of the HECM program. We already learned that the LOC will grow at the compounding rate (interest rate plus 0.5%), but the LOC also grows when making payments. Many have argued that only the portion of the payment that is applied to the principal will increase the borrower's LOC. They are mistaken. The available LOC is calculated so that any reduction in loan balance will have a corresponding increase in LOC.

POSSIBLE TAX BENEFIT

For accounting and tax purposes, a portion of the payment may be allocated toward mortgage insurance and mortgage interest. This might have beneficial tax considerations, and the loan servicer will be required to issue a Form 1098 in January, following a calendar year in which payments were made.

Chapter 35

What is HECM FOR PURCHASE?

The HECM for Purchase program was established in 2008, but homeowners are still unaware of this option. Before this program, a retired homeowner looking to relocate had to purchase a home though traditional means, establish residency, and then refinance with a HECM if desired. This included two sets of closing costs and a waiting period. It was expensive and time-consuming. Now, homebuyers can purchase a residence using a HECM with one closing and no waiting period.[56]

With a HECM for Purchase, the lender can provide a borrower with a principal limit that can be used to purchase a new home. A sizable monetary investment may be required to satisfy the remainder of the sales price and closing costs. While this downpayment might seem high, a borrower will generally invest funds from the sale of their existing residence.

The following diagram is a graphical illustration of an upsize to a more expensive home:

HECM for Purchase: Upsize

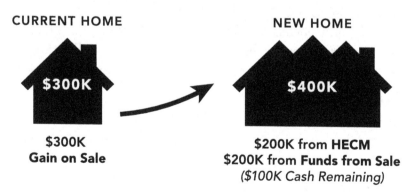

CURRENT HOME

NEW HOME

$300K

$400K

$300K
Gain on Sale

$200K from **HECM**
$200K from **Funds from Sale**
($100K Cash Remaining)

Alternately, a homeowner may be selling their current home to relocate, downsize, or "rightsize" to something more manageable, as shown in the following diagram:

HECM for Purchase: Downsize

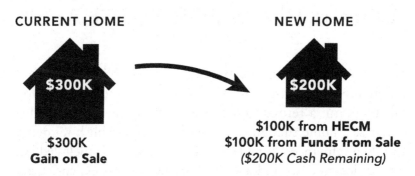

CURRENT HOME

$300K

$300K
Gain on Sale

NEW HOME

$200K

$100K from **HECM**
$100K from **Funds from Sale**
($200K Cash Remaining)

In this case, downsizing using a HECM for Purchase leaves the borrower with significant funds left over ($200,000), which can be used to supplement retirement savings.

OCCUPANCY
HECM for Purchases are only available for a borrower's "principal residence," and HUD will require the borrower to occupy the home within 60 days.

SALES CONTRACT
The lender may require the sales contract to be fully executed before an application is taken, and will request either an original copy of the sales contract or one that has every page stamped "true and certified."

SELLER-PAID CLOSING COSTS
This is an area where many mistakes are made. While HUD is now allowing certain items to be paid by the seller, the guidelines are still very restrictive regarding any type of seller contribution or concession.

HECM COUNSELING
The counseling certificate should reflect the borrower's current address, not the home that is being considered, as the subject property may change.

DISPOSAL OF THE EXISTING HOME
If the borrower wants to retain the home, they will need to show that they have sufficient funds to pay the existing home's property charges as well as the new home's property charges.

Chapter 36

How will a HECM
affect my TAXES?

Tax concerns come up frequently in training conversations. Keep in mind, I am not a tax planner, a CPA, or a financial planner, and rules regarding these items are subject to change. I can give some general guidelines, but each borrower will want to discuss these matters with a tax specialist.

Funds received through a HECM are not considered income and are therefore not taxable as such. However, if funds are drawn and placed into a bank account, they become an asset where interest can be earned. Any interest received from a new, or higher, bank account may be taxable.

On the flip side, there may be certain cases where mortgage insurance or mortgage interest that is paid on a HECM balance may be deductible, as with a traditional mortgage. With the recent tax law changes, however, the loan debt must be attributed to the acquisition or substantial improvement of the home.

Remember, HECMs do not require payments. So interest will accrue but is not "paid." I am not aware of any deductions that exist unless funds are applied to an item that is considered a deduction.

WHY DID I GET AN IRS FORM 1098?

Does this mean the homeowners owe taxes? No. But this does create some confusion for reverse mortgage borrowers every January, because loan servicers are required to notify a borrower when prepayments exceed $600.

Most reverse mortgage borrowers won't get a 1098 simply because they don't make prepayments toward their loan balances. But some will, and those borrowers need to know that the IRS Form 1098 lists items that were paid. This is for tax and accounting purposes, and it does not increase their tax liability. For our purposes, it means that borrowers made prepayments during the previous year that were applied to either their accrued mortgage insurance and/or their accrued mortgage interest.

Keep in mind, the IRS deduction for mortgage insurance must be renewed from year to year. The IRS deduction for mortgage interest, may be deductible in some cases. But of course that will depend on other factors that borrowers should discuss with their tax professionals.

Chapter 37

Will a reverse mortgage affect my GOVERNMENT BENEFITS?

I can offer general guidelines on this topic, but borrowers will want to discuss these matters with a federal benefits administrator.

Yes, a HECM can adversely affect a homeowner's government benefits. Accessing a large sum of cash from home equity and placing it in a bank account might be a problem for certain benefit programs that are "means-tested." A means test is a way of determining whether someone is eligible for assistance. If an individual has the means to do without the assistance, they may not be eligible to receive it. So, it depends on the answers to two questions:

- **Is the government benefit affected by means testing?**
- **Does the amount drawn on a monthly basis exceed the benefit's limits?**

If Mrs. Smith draws $50,000 and places the funds in her bank account, she might disqualify herself from a benefit program.

SOCIAL SECURITY AND MEDICARE

Basic Social Security is not currently means-tested, and only a portion of Medicare is based on Modified Adjusted Gross Income (MAGI). Therefore, reverse mortgage proceeds generally do not adversely affect Social Security and Medicare.

Can the reverse mortgage improve a homeowner's Social Security? Maybe. Some have used distributions from a reverse mortgage to delay filing for Social Security. The advantage is that filing as late as age 70 will increase the monthly benefit amount.

The CFPB has cautioned that those considering this strategy must weigh the costs as well as the benefits. And while this may make sense for some individuals with a periodic need for cash, the borrower should meet with a financial planner to determine if this is likely to improve their retirement cash flow.

Can a reverse mortgage improve a homeowner's Medicare Premium Surcharges? Maybe. Draws from home equity instead of other taxable sources may allow a homeowner to reduce their MAGI, which is used to determine Medicare premium surcharges for the following tax year.

SUPPLEMENTAL SECURITY AND MEDICAID

Supplemental Security and Medicaid have income and asset requirements. It will be important to know what amount held in a bank account could prevent one from receiving that assistance.

Remember, it is always a best practice for a homeowner to consult with a benefit administrator or advisor to make sure they are not jeopardizing their financial plan.

Chapter 38

How much EQUITY
is needed to QUALIFY?

A common misconception is that the home must be paid off to obtain a reverse mortgage. Others will say that one must have a large amount of equity in the home. Neither is true. Most borrowers are paying off significant liens. In fact, a homeowner can even owe more than their home is worth, sometimes described as being "upside-down," and still qualify for a HECM. They would simply need to bring funds to closing. Furthermore, those who purchase a home with a reverse mortgage have no equity at all until they bring an initial investment to closing.

One way to look at needed equity is to subtract the amount lenders can offer (the PLF %) from the maximum claim amount (100%). For example, if a 68 year old with an expected rate of 4.875% qualifies for a PLF of 46%, it would help if the borrower has 54% (100% minus 46%) in equity.

But when the principal limit is not sufficient to pay off all the homeowner's mandatory obligations, they are what is called "short to close." In such cases, the borrower must bring funds to closing.

Consider a borrower who has a $2,000 monthly forward mortgage payment and is only $1,000 short to close with the new reverse mortgage. The reverse mortgage could still make sense. For just one-half of the next scheduled payment, the borrower can obtain a reverse mortgage and no longer have to make monthly principal and interest mortgage payments.

For many HECM applicants, cash is scarce. So the more appropriate question to ask is, "How much home equity do I need so that I won't need to bring money to closing?" Unfortunately, we won't know for sure until the home's appraisal is complete. At application, we cannot tell precisely how much equity a homeowner may have and whether they will be short to close.

However, when the appraisal is completed and the expected rate is locked, we'll know the homeowner's principal limit. We can then use the following formula:

Principal Limit
(This represents the homeowner's accessible funds.)

– Mandatory Obligations
(These are items that must be paid off at closing.)

= Net Principal Limit
(This is what is left over.)

This net principal limit is what is leftover and will tell us if the borrower will need to bring money to closing.

Chapter 39

Does home EQUITY
DECREASE with a HECM?

Not necessarily. Home equity is defined as home value minus home-related debt. Whether a homeowner loses equity depends on many factors, including home appreciation rates, voluntary prepayments, and borrower draw patterns.

HOME APPRECIATION

While the housing market has had turbulent years, it's still a safe assumption that home values will increase. However, if a homeowner is concerned about depreciation, that would be a good reason to get a reverse mortgage—the funds left in the LOC will grow regardless.

Nevertheless, the more important question is whether the increase in value will outpace interest and mortgage insurance accruals.

PREPAYMENTS

As we've discussed, voluntary prepayments have advantages. Many HECM borrowers will make payments to increase their LOC, reduce their loan balance, and increase their home equity.

DRAW PATTERNS

Reverse mortgages are not designed to provide a borrower access to all their equity. Remember, a borrower's PLFs determine what percentage of a home's value may be accessed.

In addition, HUD regulations limit how much of the principal limit HECM borrowers can tap during the initial disbursement period. So, unless borrowers are paying off sizable loan balances, they may be limited to 60% of the principal limit upfront.

WHAT DO THE NUMBERS SAY?

Consider this average borrower scenario:

- A home value of $400,000
- An interest rate of 4.00% (Note: FHA adds 0.50% in MIP)
- A 74-year-old borrower with a 53.9% PLF

Home appreciation of 4% is considered a standard historic average. Therefore, 4% growth on a $400,000 home value is **$16,000**.

The borrower's principal limit is $215,600 (53.9%). Consequently, if the borrower could use 100% of their principal limit upfront, monthly compounding of an annual rate of 4.5% on a loan balance of $215,600 would be approximately **$9,905**.

First year gain in equity ➤ **$16,000 – $9,905 = $6,095**

However, if the borrower has initial disbursement limits of 60%, the interest and MIP accruals for the first year would only be $5,943, resulting in a $10,057 first year gain in equity.

Of course, the borrower is free to make voluntary prepayments to decrease the loan balance, increase the line of credit and further increase home equity.

The lesson to be learned here is that growth rates are less important than the amounts to which they are applied. Even though loan compounding is higher (4.5%), the home appreciation rate (4%) causes the borrower's equity to improve.

Chapter 40

Why not WAIT until I NEED

a reverse mortgage?

When a homeowner delays getting a reverse mortgage, there are three things that work in their favor:

1. **The borrower is getting older,** which often results in higher PLFs.

2. **The home generally appreciates,** resulting in higher principal limits.

3. **The existing mortgage balance gets smaller,** resulting in higher net principal limits.

While these three items indicate it might make sense to wait, they are generally small factors. Consider the following 67-year-old homeowner who wishes to wait until he or she is 68:

AGE	PLF (at 4%)	PLF Gain
67	50.4%	
68	51.1%	0.7%

Assuming interest rates remain at a low 4%, waiting one year would yield a PLF increase of 0.7%.

If the home appreciates by 4% during this time, the homeowner would have access to 51.1% of that appreciation by waiting. Another way to express this is a home appreciation gain of 2.04% (51.1% of 4%). This net gain of 2.74% is nice, but it's small when compared with the following factors that may negate these advantages.

THE COSTS OF WAITING

1. Expected rates are not guaranteed to stay low.
Reverse mortgage proceeds are based on long-term interest rates, and when these rates go up, new applicants may have access to less of their home equity.

2. Waiting sacrifices compounded LOC growth.
LOC growth is maximized by obtaining the reverse mortgage early and letting time do its work.

3. There is no guarantee of qualifying in the future.
Financial Assessment has made it harder to obtain a reverse mortgage at a time when you are more likely to need it.

WHAT IF INTEREST RATES GO UP?

In the example above, we established that a 67-year-old borrower with an expected interest rate rounding to 4% may qualify for 50.4% of their maximum claim amount. If rates increase even 1% while waiting, the PLF factor decreases significantly to 44.5%.

AGE	PLF (at 4%)	PLF (at 5%)	PLF (at 6%)
67	50.4%		
68	51.1%	44.5%	40.2%
	Loss	**5.9%**	**10.2%**

If long-term rates rise to 6% while waiting, that could decrease PLFs by 10.2%.

If the HECM had been secured at age 67, rising interest rates could be beneficial if that homeowner holds most of his or her funds in the growing LOC.

While we don't want to create an unmerited sense of urgency, clients need to be aware that research shows that waiting for a reverse mortgage generally isn't optimal.[57]

Chapter 41

Who is the IDEAL
reverse mortgage candidate?

Reverse mortgages are often described as a product that is not for everyone. Sadly, many perfect candidates won't consider a reverse mortgage because misinformed advisors have painted the wrong picture of the product.

Some phrases that inaccurately describe the model applicant include:

- Older homeowner
- Cash-strapped or desperate
- Seeking a last resort
- House rich, cash poor

These may be descriptions of traditional, needs-based borrowers, but with recent regulatory reforms, these borrowers are now a smaller piece of the pie.

With any reverse mortgage applicant, we want to make sure it is their intention to remain in their home. However, the following may be qualities of a great reverse mortgage candidate today:

- Age 62
- Still working
- Has about five years to pay on their forward mortgage
- May never need to access the funds

Let's look at each characteristic and why the product may be advantageous to them:

AGE 62

This is the earliest age that a borrower can qualify for a HECM, and obtaining one early maximizes the LOC growth potential. The available funds may grow at 5% annually (compounded monthly). At that rate, a $200,000 LOC would grow to nearly $600,000 in 20 years, revealing many strategic options at age 82.

STILL WORKING

Many claim the greatest advantage of a HECM is that no monthly principal or interest payments are required. I would counter that for those who are still working, the ability to make optional payments is a greater advantage. The reverse mortgage loan balance will drop similar to a forward mortgage, but each payment boosts the LOC for future use.

HAS ABOUT FIVE YEARS
TO PAY ON THEIR FORWARD MORTGAGE

Ideally, the borrower would make payments during the first few years to reduce the loan balance. If such payments can reduce the loan to a point where interest-rate adjustments are insignificant, the homeowner will benefit from higher future interest rates, as the available LOC will grow faster.

MAY NEVER NEED TO ACCESS THE FUNDS

The LOC works very well as an emergency fund, a stand-by, or even an insurance policy. While there are initial costs, the on-going costs of the loan are based on the funds that are borrowed. In other words, if the borrower never needs the funds, the carrying costs of the growing LOC may be very low.

Chapter 42

What are advanced

FINANCIAL PLANNING options?

Many with well-funded retirement plans are taking a closer look at reverse mortgages. Thanks in part to the American College of Financial Services, the financial planning community has begun to realize that HECMs can be useful in many ways.

LONG-TERM CAPITAL GAINS

Under current tax guidelines, it's possible not to pay federal income tax on capital gains if the taxpayer can stay in a lower tax bracket. One way to accomplish this is to strategically draw funds from non-taxable sources, like HECMs.

LONG-TERM CARE (LTC)

Many who don't qualify for, or who can't afford, LTC insurance may be good candidates for HECMs. Some plan to use the growing LOC to fund future in-home care, while others will use it to pay premiums on existing policies.

SILVER DIVORCE

The HECM can be useful when dividing assets in the event of divorce. In some cases, the departing spouse will want their share of the home equity. This can be accomplished without disrupting traditional retirement plans.

INSURANCE PREMIUMS

With the growing LOC as an emergency reserve, homeowners can raise their deductibles on certain insurance policies. Essentially, they can self-insure, reducing expenses and raising monthly cash flow.

SEQUENCE OF RETURNS RISK
Poor market returns early in retirement can be devastating to a portfolio. Drawing from home equity will protect traditional retirement assets and allow them to recover.

PORTFOLIO MANAGEMENT
During bull markets, some homeowners can use their market gains to pay down HECM balances. Conversely, during bear markets, they can draw from their equity to take pressure off retirement portfolios. Ultimately, they can draw less because the distributions are tax free.

RELOCATION WITH LIQUIDITY
Many baby boomers hold a disproportionate amount of their wealth in real estate. Therefore, some who wish to relocate, upsize, or downsize can keep more cash in the bank by using a HECM for Purchase.

RETIREMENT GOALS
Many pre-retirees are faced with a decision: Should I accelerate payments on my forward mortgage to reduce my balance, or should I save funds for retirement? Making payments with a HECM can accomplish both objectives.

Chapter 43

What are PROPRIETARY

REVERSE MORTGAGES?

The federally insured HECM has been the dominant reverse mortgage product for the last three decades. That is changing, however, as innovative mortgage lenders have found that certain restrictive HECM guidelines have opened the door for non-agency reverse mortgage products.

These "proprietary" reverse mortgage options still maintain many of the consumer protections of the HECM program. Reverse mortgages, FHA-insured or not, must be non-recourse loans. But, of course, these proprietary products do not charge the initial MIP (2%) or annual MIP (0.5%). So, while the rates may be slightly higher, you might find the up-front charges to be significantly reduced.

For the last few years the phrase "jumbo reverse mortgage" was used to describe these options, as lenders were able to better serve borrowers who owned higher-priced homes.

However, these new products solve other problems that HECMs currently do not. Here are a few:

- HECMs require condominium units to be FHA approved before they can be eligible for HECM financing. Proprietary products may finance units within condos that are not FHA-approved.

- HECMs have initial disbursement limits that often prevent borrowers from accessing more than 60% of their principal limit within the first year. Proprietary products have no such restrictions.

- HECMs require all existing liens to be paid off a closing. Proprietary products may allow the reverse mortgage to be in second lien position.

- HECMs do not currently allow the payoff of unsecured debt at closing. Proprietary products may allow the payoff of personal debt and other items at closing.

- HECMs require most liens to be seasoned for 12 months before closing. Proprietary products may have relaxed seasoning requirements.

- HECMs require all borrowers to be age 62 or older. Proprietary products may offer financing for younger borrowers.

Some are offered as first liens. Some are structured with a growing line of credit that mimics the HECM ARM. Still others, as noted above, can remain in a second-lien position in cases where the first mortgage has an attractive low rate.

Not all proprietary reverse mortgage products are the same. They each offer various features that may appeal to different homeowners. If interested, make sure to inquire about state availability. These new products must be approved in every state where the product will be offered, and no lender has nationwide coverage for their proprietary products.

Chapter 44

What should I expect during SERVICING?

Every HECM must be serviced according to HUD guidelines, but not all lenders service their own loans. The following are common questions related to servicing:

WHY DID I GET AN OCCUPANCY CERTIFICATION?

Reverse mortgages are only offered for primary residences. Therefore, the homeowner must certify their occupancy of the property (via mail) one year after closing and every year thereafter. This is not an inspection of the property, and home-owners should not feel that this is a violation of their privacy. The homeowner simply returns the signed certification indicating they still meet the requirements of the program. If the letter is not returned, the servicer may be required to follow up with phone calls and possibly a visit to the property.[58]

WILL I GET A MONTHLY STATEMENT?

Yes. Borrowers receive an activity statement so they can keep track of their loan balances and their available lines of credit.

HOW ARE PREPAYMENTS APPLIED?

One of the primary financial planning strategies is making periodic prepayments. The result should be a reduction in the loan balance, and a corresponding increase to the borrower's available line of credit. When payments are made, however, they are applied to different accounting buckets in a progression known as the servicing waterfall shown here:[59]

1st – Accrued mortgage insurance (IMIP and MIP)
2nd – Servicing fees (if charged)
3rd – Interest accruals
4th – Principal

This means that homeowners will have to pay back all their accrued mortgage insurance before they will be eligible for a potential mortgage interest deduction.

The servicing waterfall is only important for tax and accounting purposes, and it should not impact the borrower's ability to draw those prepaid funds again. Any reduction in loan balance should increase the available LOC.

WHY IS HUD SERVICING MY LOAN?

HECM loans may be assigned to HUD for many reasons. The most common is the loan balance approaching the maximum claim amount (MCA). Lenders/servicers can assign a loan to HUD when a loan balance (or a request for funds) reaches 98% of the MCA.[60]

Documents are signed at closing that also allow HUD to service the loan when the lender is unable to distribute the required funds to the borrower. While lenders/servicers are unlikely to go out of business while maintaining a servicing portfolio, it is nice to know that HUD will ensure homeowners are protected.

Chapter 45

What is necessary
to PAY OFF a HECM?

The conventional wisdom is that a HECM payoff will be the lesser of the loan balance or 95% of the property's appraised value. Unfortunately, this is only true under certain circumstances.

Consider an older borrower whose financial position has changed. Maybe it was a life insurance claim for a deceased spouse, inherited funds, or an investment that matured. Whatever the reason, if that borrower wishes to payoff a HECM loan balance, they owe the full loan balance.

There are cases, however, where borrowers or their heirs can satisfy the HECM for 95% of the appraised value. The availability of this option may depend on whether the loan is *"due and payable,"* who is doing the satisfying, and the definition of the word *"sale."*

WITH A TRADITIONAL SALE OF THE PROPERTY

The borrower or their estate may sell the property at any time for the lesser of the following two values:

1. The debt due under the mortgage, or
2. The appraised value at the time of the sale.[61]

Therefore, one CANNOT arbitrarily sell the home for 95% of the appraised value and satisfy a HECM loan balance that exceeds this amount.

WHEN THE LOAN IS DUE AND PAYABLE

If the mortgage is due and payable at the time the contract for sale is executed, the threshold is reduced. This is generally the case when the last borrower has died. In this event, the estate may sell the property for the lesser of the loan balance or 95% of the current appraised value.[62]

In essence, the "95% SALE" option becomes available when the HECM loan becomes due and payable.

IF THE HEIRS WANT TO KEEP THE PROPERTY

This can get tricky. The non-recourse feature offered with reverse mortgages requires a sale of the home. Fortunately, HUD interprets the word "sale" to include any post-death conveyance of the property to the borrower's estate or heirs.[63]

Therefore, if the heirs want to keep the home and want a discounted payoff of the HECM loan balance, they will need to show a transfer of title that occurs upon the death of the last borrower, or after. This could be in the form of a trust, a life estate, or simply probating the homeowner's will.

The danger is that heirs who are already on title at the time of the last borrower's death may not qualify for the reduced payoff.

Chapter 46

What are some HELPFUL HINTS
and RED FLAGS?

THERE IS A THREE-DAY RIGHT OF RESCISSION.
"Closing" and "funding" are not the same, so don't panic when funds are not in the account right away. Most HECMs are refinances and therefore have a three-day right of rescission.[64] This means that within three days of closing, a homeowner can opt-out of the transaction. Because of bank wiring times and weekends, borrowers should expect to see the funds in their account within one week of closing.

LOWER INTEREST RATES ARE NOT ALWAYS BEST.
There are circumstances under which a borrower might be better served by a higher rate. This happens quite frequently. The following are three reasons why this is true:

1. Lender credits
At higher rates, lenders or brokers may be able to offer credits toward closing costs. If the objective is to keep the loan balance low in the short-run, it might be advantageous to accept a higher rate and reduce the costs.

2. Higher LOC growth
Remember, the available LOC will grow at the interest rate plus 0.5%. If a borrower is carrying a low loan balance of $100, an extra 1% is only costing them an additional $1 per year in interest. Meanwhile, an LOC of $200,000 will grow by approximately $2,000 more.

3. Higher tenure payments
The expected rate (ER) is used to calculate the borrower's principal limit. But it is also used to calculate tenure payments. In some cases, higher ERs may convert to higher monthly payouts.

Some say that if the borrower chooses an LOC, the tenure advantage doesn't exist. That is not true. Many years later, if the borrower converts the growing LOC into a tenure payment, the servicing department will "annuitize" the net principal limit using the only expected rate in the system—the one established at closing.

WHEN IS YOUR NEXT BIRTHDAY?

The timing of the closing can impact how much the homeowner receives. This is because FHA uses whole ages (the nearest age) to determine principal limits. Therefore, if the youngest participant is within six months of his/her next birthday, FHA rounds up, and the borrower may qualify for more funds. If the homeowner is short to close by a just little, timing the closing might provide the additional funds.

YOUR BROKER/LENDER CANNOT REQUIRE YOU TO BUY OTHER PRODUCTS.

Reverse mortgage professionals cannot require clients to buy annuities, investments, or any other financial instruments as a condition for getting a HECM.[65] Although rare, if this does occur, you may file a complaint with the Consumer Financial Protection Bureau.

FHA MAY REQUIRE A 2ND APPRAISAL[66]

To ensure that appraisals are accurate, FHA has implemented an internal appraisal review called "Collateral Risk Assessment." Most appraisals will be fine. However, if FHA flags the appraisal, a second appraisal will be required. The new appraisal will either confirm the original value or reduce the value. Because the cost of the average appraisal exceeds $500, this is a potential cost the loan originator and borrower should discuss upfront.

Chapter 47

What are the NEXT STEPS?

I wrote this book to help people better understand reverse mortgages. Hopefully, the terms of the HECM program are now more familiar. But leveraging your hard-earned home equity can still be a difficult choice.

For you, your heirs, or your reverse mortgage professional, this is not something to take lightly. You should never feel pressured into a decision. The best loan originators are educators, not salespeople. So, take your time, develop a relationship with an experienced HECM professional, and make the right choice for you and your family.

You have taken the first step by choosing to educate yourself. Nevertheless, here is a 10-step process that may help as you move forward:

1. Initial Discussion
Review the HECM product with a reverse mortgage professional who is licensed in your area. While some forward mortgage professionals understand the intricacies involved in originating HECMs, others don't.

2. Pre-Counseling Package
Obtain this information from your loan originator. It should include the following documentation:

- Counseling list that includes numbers for national and local agencies
- Loan comparison of various product options
- Total Annual Loan Cost (TALC) rate disclosure
- Amortization schedule
- *Use Your Home to Stay at Home* booklet from the NCOA

3. Counseling
Complete a counseling session with a HUD-approved counselor and bring along family members or other interested parties. The counselor will send certificates that must be signed and dated by all participants. The lender is restricted in what they can do until a fully signed and dated counseling certificate is provided.

4. Loan Application
Contact your chosen HECM specialist to complete the application, which is called a Form 1009. Additional disclosures will need to be signed at that time.

5. Appraisal
An appraiser will visit your home to take pictures and measurements. They will generate a report of comparable sales, which will be used by the underwriter to determine the current value of the home.

6. Processing
A processor will likely contact you to collect additional information necessary to send the loan file to an underwriter.

7. Underwriting
The underwriter is the final decision-maker regarding critical elements of the loan and makes sure that the loan file is in order.

8. Closing
When the loan is approved by the underwriter, it may be cleared to close and closing will be scheduled.

9. Servicing
When closed, your loan will be managed by one of only a handful of loan servicers that specialize in HECM loans.

10. *Last, please recommend this book to your friends, family, and neighbors.*

KEY TERMS

ADJUSTABLE-RATE HECM (HECM ARM): A loan with a variable rate that changes monthly or annually and is tied to the movements of a published index.

CAP: A limit on the amount that a variable interest rate may increase or decrease during a specified time. The capped rate will be listed in the note.

CERTIFIED REVERSE MORTGAGE PROFESSIONAL (CRMP): This designation, administered by the National Reverse Mortgage Lenders Association, requires testing and regular continuing education.

EXPECTED RATE (ER): An anticipated interest rate that is used to determine the principal limit on a HECM loan. On a fixed-rate HECM, the expected rate is the same as the interest rate. With the HECM ARM, the expected rate equals a 10-year index plus the lender margin.

FEDERAL HOUSING ADMINISTRATION (FHA): An agency within the U.S. Department of Housing and Urban Development (HUD) that issues insurance to private lenders for forward and reverse mortgage loans

FINANCIAL ASSESSMENT: A HECM program guideline that requires an underwriter to assess credit history, property charge payment history, and monthly residual income to determine the loan's sustainability for each borrower. In many cases, the underwriter will require funds to be set aside to pay for critical property charges.

FIXED-RATE HECM: A reverse mortgage with rates that do not change during the life of the loan; often referred to as the HECM Fixed

HECM (HOME EQUITY CONVERSION MORTGAGE): Commonly referred to as a reverse mortgage, this FHA-insured program is designed to enable homeowners, age 62 and over, to convert a portion of the equity in their home into cash and/or lines of credit.

HECM FOR PURCHASE (H4P): A program for homebuyers 62 and older that allows them to purchase a new home with no required monthly principal or interest mortgage payments. Title to the property is transferred to the new mortgagor, who must occupy the property as a primary residence within 60 days of the closing.

HECM TO HECM REFI (H2H REFI): A reverse mortgage variation that allows current HECM borrowers to refinance into a new HECM loan

HUD: The U.S. Department of Housing and Urban Development, a federal agency that oversees the Federal Housing Administration and numerous housing and community development programs

INITIAL DISBURSEMENT LIMIT: A limit to how much a HECM borrower can withdraw at closing (for a HECM Fixed) or during the first year (for a HECM ARM). The limit will be the greater of 60% of the principal limit or the mandatory obligations plus 10% of the principal limit.

INITIAL MORTGAGE INSURANCE PREMIUM (IMIP): Also called up-front MIP, this is 2% of the maximum claim amount and is paid to the federal government for insuring the loan.

LIEN SEASONING: Borrowers may only pay off existing non-HECM liens using HECM proceeds if the liens had been in place longer than 12 months or resulted in less than $500 cash to the borrower. An exception exists for HELOCs where the payoff is within the borrowers first year disbursement limit.

LIFE EXPECTANCY SET-ASIDE (LESA): Funds that are removed from a borrower's principal limit and set aside for the payment of property charges over a calculated time. A LESA is established when the underwriter determines that a borrower fails to pass a Financial Assessment test.

LINE OF CREDIT (LOC): When the borrower does not access all of their principal limit, the remainder may be available in a credit line. This popular payout option is available for adjustable-rate HECMs only. LOC funds will grow, will be secure, and will be available for future use, but will not accrue interest or mortgage insurance charges.

MANDATORY OBLIGATIONS: Items that must be paid off at closing or during the initial disbursement period. These include mortgages, liens, judgments that affect the home's title, federal debt, closing costs, and initial mortgage insurance premiums. If the loan requires a LESA, this could also include property taxes and insurance due in the first year. Mandatory obligations may be financed into the loan or paid by the homeowner at closing.

MARGIN (LENDER MARGIN): For HECM ARMs, the margin is a percentage added to the index, and the combination of the two numbers will equal the current interest rate. For example, if the lender margin is 2% and the index is 2%, the resulting interest rate would be 4%. The margin portion of the interest rate never changes over the life of the loan.

MAXIMUM CLAIM AMOUNT (MCA): This is generally the lesser of the home's value or the nationwide HECM limit. Loans can be originated on homes valued over this threshold, but a homeowner's available funds will be calculated as if the home was valued at the limit.

MODIFIED TENURE: A combination of tenure payments and a line of credit

MODIFIED TERM: A combination of term payments and a line of credit

MORTGAGE INSURANCE PREMIUM (MIP): Insurance premiums on a HECM loan, which are collected in two forms: initial MIP (IMIP) collected at closing and annual MIP. Most clients will finance both as part of their HECM loan balance.

MORTGAGEE: A term often used in HECM guidelines and federal regulations that refers to the mortgage lender

MORTGAGOR: Anyone who remains on title to the home. This must include the borrower, but may also include a non-borrowing spouse or other co-owner of the home, even though they may not qualify as a HECM borrower.

NATIONAL REVERSE MORTGAGE LENDERS ASSOCIATION (NRMLA): A trade association that is the national voice of the reverse mortgage industry, serving as an educational resource, policy advocate, and public affairs center for lenders and related professionals

NON-BORROWING SPOUSE (NBS): The spouse of a HECM borrower who is not a borrower, most commonly because they are not of qualifying age

NON-RECOURSE FEATURE: A feature of a reverse mortgage loan that dictates that a borrower and their heirs will not owe more than the home is worth at the time it is sold

ORIGINATION FEE: A one-time fee paid to the lender at closing. For HECMs, the maximum origination fee is 2% on the initial $200,000 in home value, and 1% on the value thereafter with a cap of $6,000. FHA allows a minimum of $2,500 regardless of value.

PRIMARY RESIDENCE (PRINCIPAL RESIDENCE): A home occupied by its owner for more than 50% of the year. A reverse mortgage may only be obtained on a primary residence, or a residence that will become primary within 60 days.

PRINCIPAL LIMIT: The amount of money a reverse mortgage borrower can receive. The principal limit is calculated by multiplying the borrower's maximum claim amount by the principal limit factor (PLF). With this amount, the lender will pay off mortgages or liens that affect title, delinquent federal debt, and any costs associated with the loan. The remainder is called the net principal limit (NPL).

PRINCIPAL LIMIT FACTORS (PLFS): The percent of the maximum claim amount that a reverse mortgage borrower can access given their age and the loan's expected rate. PLF tables are published by HUD and determine how much a lender can offer a homeowner.

REVERSE MORTGAGE: A financial tool that provides homeowners with funds from the equity in their homes. Generally, no principal or interest payments are made on reverse mortgages until the borrower moves or the property is sold.

TENURE PAYMENT: A payout option on HECM ARM products that allows a borrower to receive equal monthly payments for as long as they occupy the home and abide by program guidelines. The borrower will continue to receive funds with this option regardless of how long they live, even if their home value declines.

TERM PAYMENT: A payout option on HECM ARMs that allows a borrower to receive equal monthly payments for a fixed number of months. Longer terms offer the borrower smaller payments, while shorter terms offer the borrower larger payments.

Principal Limit Factors
QUICK REFERENCE GUIDE

HECM principal limit factor (PLF) tables are published by HUD and change periodically. When this book was published, the most recent table was released October 2, 2017.

PLFs are based on the relevant age and the expected rate of the HECM loan. The **relevant age** is the nearest age of the youngest borrower (or eligible non-borrowing spouse) at the time of closing. Therefore, if the closing date is set within six months of that individual's next birthday, the age will be rounded up. Consequently, the borrower will qualify for more funds.

For PLF purposes, the **expected rate** is rounded to the nearest 1/8%. For example, 5.06% rounds down to 5% when referencing the table. 5.07% would round up to 5.125%, and the borrower would generally qualify for less funds.

By knowing the relevant age and rate, you can use this handy reference sheet to quickly see the maximum percentage of a home's value a lender may currently offer a borrower.

The full PLF tables begin at 3% and change every 0.125% up to 18.875%. However, the following quick reference guide only displays commonly used expected rates between 3% and 5.875%. You will also notice that this guide has excluded the PLFs for non-borrowing spouses below age 45.

CHART 1: For borrowers and spouses who are already 62 or older

Age	3%	3.125%	3.25%	3.375%	3.50%	3.625%	3.75%	3.875%
62	52.4%	52.4%	52.2%	51.3%	50.4%	49.6%	48.7%	47.9%
63	53.0%	53.0%	52.8%	51.9%	51.1%	50.2%	49.3%	48.5%
64	53.6%	53.6%	53.4%	52.6%	51.7%	50.8%	50.0%	49.2%
65	54.2%	54.2%	54.0%	53.2%	52.3%	51.5%	50.6%	49.8%
66	54.9%	54.9%	54.7%	53.8%	52.9%	52.1%	51.3%	50.5%
67	55.6%	55.6%	55.3%	54.5%	53.6%	52.8%	52.0%	51.2%
68	56.2%	56.2%	56.0%	55.1%	54.3%	53.5%	52.7%	51.9%
69	56.9%	56.9%	56.6%	55.8%	55.0%	54.2%	53.4%	52.6%
70	57.6%	57.6%	57.0%	56.2%	55.4%	54.6%	53.8%	53.0%
71	58.3%	57.8%	57.0%	56.2%	55.4%	54.6%	53.8%	53.0%
72	58.8%	58.0%	57.2%	56.3%	55.5%	54.7%	53.9%	53.1%
73	59.5%	58.7%	57.9%	57.0%	56.2%	55.5%	54.7%	53.9%
74	60.2%	59.3%	58.5%	57.7%	56.9%	56.1%	55.4%	54.6%
75	60.9%	60.1%	59.3%	58.5%	57.7%	56.9%	56.2%	55.5%
76	61.4%	60.6%	59.8%	59.0%	58.2%	57.5%	56.7%	56.0%
77	62.1%	61.3%	60.6%	59.8%	59.1%	58.3%	57.6%	56.9%
78	62.9%	62.1%	61.4%	60.6%	59.9%	59.2%	58.5%	57.8%
79	63.3%	62.6%	61.8%	61.1%	60.4%	59.7%	58.9%	58.2%
80	64.2%	63.4%	62.7%	62.0%	61.3%	60.6%	59.9%	59.2%
81	65.0%	64.3%	63.6%	62.9%	62.2%	61.5%	60.8%	60.1%
82	65.8%	65.1%	64.4%	63.8%	63.1%	62.4%	61.8%	61.1%
83	66.7%	66.0%	65.3%	64.7%	64.0%	63.4%	62.7%	62.1%
84	67.6%	66.9%	66.3%	65.6%	65.0%	64.4%	63.7%	63.1%
85	68.5%	67.8%	67.2%	66.6%	66.0%	65.4%	64.8%	64.2%
86	69.4%	68.8%	68.2%	67.6%	67.0%	66.4%	65.8%	65.2%
87	70.3%	69.7%	69.1%	68.6%	68.0%	67.4%	66.9%	66.3%
88	71.1%	70.5%	70.0%	69.4%	68.9%	68.3%	67.8%	67.2%
89	72.1%	71.5%	71.0%	70.5%	69.9%	69.4%	68.9%	68.4%
90	73.0%	72.5%	72.0%	71.5%	71.0%	70.5%	70.0%	69.5%
91	74.0%	73.6%	73.1%	72.6%	72.1%	71.7%	71.2%	70.7%
92	75.0%	74.6%	74.2%	73.7%	73.3%	72.8%	72.4%	72.0%
93	75.0%	75.0%	75.0%	74.9%	74.4%	74.0%	73.6%	73.2%
94	75.0%	75.0%	75.0%	75.0%	75.0%	75.0%	74.9%	74.5%
95	75.0%	75.0%	75.0%	75.0%	75.0%	75.0%	75.0%	75.0%
96	75.0%	75.0%	75.0%	75.0%	75.0%	75.0%	75.0%	75.0%
97	75.0%	75.0%	75.0%	75.0%	75.0%	75.0%	75.0%	75.0%
98	75.0%	75.0%	75.0%	75.0%	75.0%	75.0%	75.0%	75.0%
99	75.0%	75.0%	75.0%	75.0%	75.0%	75.0%	75.0%	75.0%

Age	4%	4.125%	4.25%	4.375%	4.50%	4.625%	4.75%	4.875%
62	47.0%	46.2%	45.4%	44.7%	43.9%	43.1%	42.4%	41.7%
63	47.7%	46.9%	46.1%	45.3%	44.6%	43.8%	43.1%	42.3%
64	48.3%	47.5%	46.8%	46.0%	45.2%	44.5%	43.8%	43.0%
65	49.0%	48.2%	47.4%	46.7%	45.9%	45.2%	44.4%	43.7%
66	49.7%	48.9%	48.1%	47.4%	46.6%	45.9%	45.2%	44.5%
67	50.4%	49.6%	48.8%	48.1%	47.3%	46.6%	45.9%	45.2%
68	51.1%	50.3%	49.6%	48.8%	48.1%	47.4%	46.7%	46.0%
69	51.8%	51.0%	50.3%	49.6%	48.8%	48.1%	47.4%	46.7%
70	52.2%	51.5%	50.7%	50.0%	49.3%	48.6%	47.9%	47.2%
71	52.2%	51.5%	50.7%	50.0%	49.3%	48.6%	47.9%	47.2%
72	52.4%	51.6%	50.9%	50.2%	49.4%	48.7%	48.0%	47.4%
73	53.2%	52.4%	51.7%	51.0%	50.3%	49.6%	48.9%	48.2%
74	53.9%	53.1%	52.4%	51.7%	51.0%	50.3%	49.6%	49.0%
75	54.7%	54.0%	53.3%	52.6%	51.9%	51.2%	50.5%	49.9%
76	55.3%	54.6%	53.9%	53.2%	52.5%	51.8%	51.1%	50.5%
77	56.2%	55.5%	54.8%	54.1%	53.4%	52.7%	52.1%	51.4%
78	57.1%	56.4%	55.7%	55.0%	54.4%	53.7%	53.1%	52.4%
79	57.6%	56.9%	56.2%	55.5%	54.9%	54.2%	53.6%	53.0%
80	58.5%	57.8%	57.2%	56.5%	55.9%	55.3%	54.6%	54.0%
81	59.5%	58.8%	58.2%	57.5%	56.9%	56.3%	55.7%	55.1%
82	60.5%	59.8%	59.2%	58.6%	58.0%	57.4%	56.8%	56.2%
83	61.5%	60.9%	60.2%	59.6%	59.0%	58.5%	57.9%	57.3%
84	62.5%	61.9%	61.3%	60.7%	60.1%	59.6%	59.0%	58.4%
85	63.6%	63.0%	62.4%	61.8%	61.3%	60.7%	60.2%	59.6%
86	64.7%	64.1%	63.5%	63.0%	62.4%	61.9%	61.4%	60.8%
87	65.8%	65.2%	64.7%	64.1%	63.6%	63.1%	62.6%	62.1%
88	66.7%	66.2%	65.7%	65.1%	64.6%	64.1%	63.6%	63.1%
89	67.9%	67.4%	66.9%	66.4%	65.9%	65.4%	64.9%	64.4%
90	69.1%	68.6%	68.1%	67.6%	67.2%	66.7%	66.2%	65.8%
91	70.3%	69.8%	69.4%	68.9%	68.5%	68.0%	67.6%	67.2%
92	71.5%	71.1%	70.7%	70.3%	69.8%	69.4%	69.0%	68.6%
93	72.8%	72.4%	72.0%	71.6%	71.2%	70.8%	70.4%	70.1%
94	74.1%	73.7%	73.4%	73.0%	72.6%	72.3%	71.9%	71.5%
95	75.0%	75.0%	74.7%	74.3%	74.0%	73.7%	73.3%	73.0%
96	75.0%	75.0%	75.0%	75.0%	74.7%	74.4%	74.1%	73.7%
97	75.0%	75.0%	75.0%	75.0%	75.0%	74.9%	74.6%	74.3%
98	75.0%	75.0%	75.0%	75.0%	75.0%	74.9%	74.6%	74.3%
99	75.0%	75.0%	75.0%	75.0%	75.0%	74.9%	74.6%	74.3%

(continued)

(continued)

CHART 1: For borrowers and spouses who are already 62 or older

Age	5%	5.125%	5.25%	5.375%	5.50%	5.625%	5.75%	5.875%
62	41.0%	40.3%	39.6%	38.9%	38.2%	37.6%	37.0%	36.3%
63	41.6%	40.9%	40.3%	39.6%	38.9%	38.3%	37.6%	37.0%
64	42.3%	41.6%	41.0%	40.3%	39.6%	39.0%	38.4%	37.7%
65	43.0%	42.3%	41.7%	41.0%	40.3%	39.7%	39.1%	38.4%
66	43.8%	43.1%	42.4%	41.7%	41.1%	40.5%	39.8%	39.2%
67	44.5%	43.8%	43.2%	42.5%	41.9%	41.2%	40.6%	40.0%
68	45.3%	44.6%	43.9%	43.3%	42.6%	42.0%	41.4%	40.8%
69	46.1%	45.4%	44.7%	44.1%	43.4%	42.8%	42.2%	41.6%
70	46.5%	45.8%	45.2%	44.5%	43.9%	43.3%	42.7%	42.0%
71	46.5%	45.8%	45.2%	44.5%	43.9%	43.3%	42.7%	42.1%
72	46.7%	46.0%	45.4%	44.7%	44.1%	43.5%	42.8%	42.2%
73	47.5%	46.9%	46.2%	45.6%	44.9%	44.3%	43.7%	43.1%
74	48.3%	47.7%	47.0%	46.4%	45.8%	45.1%	44.5%	43.9%
75	49.2%	48.6%	47.9%	47.3%	46.7%	46.1%	45.5%	44.9%
76	49.8%	49.2%	48.6%	47.9%	47.3%	46.7%	46.1%	45.5%
77	50.8%	50.2%	49.5%	48.9%	48.3%	47.7%	47.1%	46.6%
78	51.8%	51.2%	50.6%	50.0%	49.4%	48.8%	48.2%	47.6%
79	52.3%	51.7%	51.1%	50.5%	49.9%	49.4%	48.8%	48.2%
80	53.4%	52.8%	52.2%	51.6%	51.0%	50.5%	49.9%	49.3%
81	54.5%	53.9%	53.3%	52.7%	52.2%	51.6%	51.0%	50.5%
82	55.6%	55.0%	54.4%	53.9%	53.3%	52.8%	52.2%	51.7%
83	56.7%	56.2%	55.6%	55.0%	54.5%	54.0%	53.4%	52.9%
84	57.9%	57.3%	56.8%	56.2%	55.7%	55.2%	54.7%	54.1%
85	59.1%	58.5%	58.0%	57.5%	57.0%	56.4%	55.9%	55.4%
86	60.3%	59.8%	59.3%	58.8%	58.2%	57.7%	57.3%	56.8%
87	61.6%	61.1%	60.6%	60.1%	59.6%	59.1%	58.6%	58.1%
88	62.6%	62.1%	61.7%	61.2%	60.7%	60.2%	59.8%	59.3%
89	64.0%	63.5%	63.0%	62.6%	62.1%	61.7%	61.2%	60.8%
90	65.3%	64.9%	64.4%	64.0%	63.6%	63.1%	62.7%	62.3%
91	66.7%	66.3%	65.9%	65.5%	65.1%	64.6%	64.2%	63.8%
92	68.2%	67.8%	67.4%	67.0%	66.6%	66.2%	65.8%	65.4%
93	69.7%	69.3%	68.9%	68.5%	68.2%	67.8%	67.4%	67.1%
94	71.2%	70.8%	70.5%	70.1%	69.8%	69.4%	69.1%	68.8%
95	72.7%	72.3%	72.0%	71.7%	71.4%	71.0%	70.7%	70.4%
96	73.4%	73.1%	72.8%	72.5%	72.2%	71.9%	71.6%	71.3%
97	74.0%	73.7%	73.4%	73.1%	72.8%	72.5%	72.2%	71.9%
98	74.0%	73.7%	73.4%	73.1%	72.8%	72.5%	72.2%	71.9%
99	74.0%	73.7%	73.4%	73.1%	72.8%	72.5%	72.2%	71.9%

CHART 2: For eligible non-borrowing spouses (NBS) under age 62

Age	3%	3.125%	3.25%	3.375%	3.50%	3.625%	3.75%	3.875%
45	44.1%	43.0%	42.0%	41.0%	40.0%	39.0%	38.1%	37.1%
46	44.3%	43.6%	42.5%	41.5%	40.5%	39.5%	38.6%	37.7%
47	44.3%	44.1%	43.0%	42.0%	41.0%	40.1%	39.1%	38.2%
48	44.3%	44.3%	43.5%	42.5%	41.5%	40.6%	39.6%	38.7%
49	44.3%	44.3%	44.1%	43.1%	42.1%	41.1%	40.2%	39.3%
50	46.0%	45.6%	44.6%	43.6%	42.6%	41.7%	40.7%	39.8%
51	46.0%	46.0%	45.1%	44.2%	43.2%	42.2%	41.3%	40.4%
52	46.0%	46.0%	45.7%	44.7%	43.7%	42.8%	41.9%	41.0%
53	46.0%	46.0%	46.0%	45.3%	44.3%	43.4%	42.4%	41.5%
54	46.0%	46.0%	46.0%	45.8%	44.9%	43.9%	43.0%	42.1%
55	48.4%	48.4%	47.4%	46.4%	45.5%	44.5%	43.6%	42.7%
56	48.9%	48.9%	48.0%	47.0%	46.0%	45.1%	44.2%	43.3%
57	49.5%	49.5%	48.5%	47.6%	46.6%	45.7%	44.8%	43.9%
58	50.0%	50.0%	49.1%	48.2%	47.2%	46.3%	45.4%	44.6%
59	50.6%	50.6%	49.7%	48.8%	47.9%	47.0%	46.1%	45.2%
60	51.1%	51.1%	50.3%	49.4%	48.5%	47.6%	46.7%	45.8%
61	51.7%	51.7%	50.9%	50.0%	49.1%	48.2%	47.3%	46.5%

Age	4%	4.125%	4.25%	4.375%	4.50%	4.625%	4.75%	4.875%
45	36.2%	35.4%	34.5%	33.7%	32.9%	32.1%	31.3%	30.6%
46	36.8%	35.9%	35.0%	34.2%	33.4%	32.6%	31.8%	31.1%
47	37.3%	36.4%	35.6%	34.7%	33.9%	33.1%	32.4%	31.6%
48	37.8%	37.0%	36.1%	35.3%	34.5%	33.7%	32.9%	32.2%
49	38.4%	37.5%	36.7%	35.8%	35.0%	34.2%	33.5%	32.7%
50	38.9%	38.1%	37.2%	36.4%	35.6%	34.8%	34.0%	33.3%
51	39.5%	38.6%	37.8%	37.0%	36.2%	35.4%	34.6%	33.9%
52	40.1%	39.2%	38.4%	37.6%	36.8%	36.0%	35.2%	34.4%
53	40.7%	39.8%	39.0%	38.1%	37.3%	36.6%	35.8%	35.0%
54	41.3%	40.4%	39.6%	38.7%	37.9%	37.2%	36.4%	35.7%
55	41.9%	41.0%	40.2%	39.4%	38.6%	37.8%	37.0%	36.3%
56	42.5%	41.6%	40.8%	40.0%	39.2%	38.4%	37.6%	36.9%
57	43.1%	42.2%	41.4%	40.6%	39.8%	39.0%	38.3%	37.5%
58	43.7%	42.9%	42.0%	41.2%	40.5%	39.7%	38.9%	38.2%
59	44.3%	43.5%	42.7%	41.9%	41.1%	40.3%	39.6%	38.8%
60	45.0%	44.2%	43.3%	42.5%	41.8%	41.0%	40.3%	39.5%
61	45.6%	44.8%	44.0%	43.2%	42.4%	41.7%	40.9%	40.2%

REFERENCES

The following references offer further guidance about the topics covered in this book.

1. Federal Trade Commission: www.consumer.ftc.gov

If you're 62 or older – and want money to pay off your mortgage, supplement your income, or pay for healthcare expenses—you may consider a reverse mortgage. It allows you to convert part of the equity in your home into cash without having to sell your home or pay additional monthly bills.

2. Section 255 of the National Housing Act (12 U.S.C. 1715z–20)

The purpose of this section is to authorize the Secretary to carry out a program of mortgage insurance designed to meet the special needs of elderly homeowners by reducing the effect of the economic hardship caused by the increasing costs of meeting health, housing, and subsistence needs at a time of reduced income, through the insurance of home equity conversion mortgages to permit the conversion of a portion of accumulated home equity into liquid assets.

3. HUD Handbook 4235.1 Chapter 1-2

The program insures what are commonly referred to as reverse mortgages, and is designed to enable elderly homeowners to convert the equity in their homes to monthly streams of income and/or lines of credit.

4. CFPB–Report to Congress on Reverse Mortgages, June 2012

Some prospective borrowers' financial situations may be fundamentally unsustainable. Using a reverse mortgage to hold on to the home for the near term may simply postpone hard decisions, provide little long-term benefit to the borrower, and consume most or all of the borrower's home equity in the process. This type of borrower is at high risk of getting behind on taxes and insurance, and facing foreclosure on the reverse mortgage.

5. 24 CFR §206.33. AGE OF BORROWER
The youngest borrower shall be 62 years of age or older at the time of loan closing.

6. 24 CFR §206.39(a). PRINCIPAL RESIDENCE
The property must be the principal residence of each borrower, and if applicable, Eligible Non-Borrowing Spouse, at closing.

7. Mortgagee Letter 2014-21. POLICY AND DEFINITIONS
Mandatory Obligations: Fees and charges incurred in connection with the origination of the HECM that are permitted, under this Mortgagee Letter, to be:

- paid at loan closing or during the First-12 Month Disbursement Period that are a condition or a requirement for loan approval; or

- any disbursements for a Repair Set-Aside, including the cost of repairs and the repair administration fee.

8. Mortgagee Letter 2013-27.
INITIAL DISBURSEMENT LIMITS (Fixed rate payout)
The maximum disbursement allowed at loan closing is: The greater of sixty percent (60%) of the Principal Limit; or the sum of Mandatory Obligations plus ten percent of the Principal Limit.

9. Mortgagee Letter 2013-27.
INITIAL DISBURSEMENT LIMITS (ARM payout options)
The maximum disbursement allowed at loan closing and during the First 12-Month Disbursement Period is: The greater of sixty percent (60%) of the Principal Limit; or the sum of Mandatory Obligations plus ten percent of the Principal Limit.

10. 24 CFR §206.36 (a)

Such seasoning requirements shall not prohibit the payoff of existing non-HECM liens using HECM proceeds if the liens have been in place for longer than 12 months prior to the HECM closing or if the liens have resulted in cash to the borrower in an amount of $500 or less, whether at closing or through cumulative draws prior to the date of the HECM closing.

11. 24 CFR §206.36 (c)

The borrower may pay off, at closing, a Home Equity Line of Credit (HELOC) that does not meet seasoning requirements from borrower funds, the HECM funds, or a combination of HECM funds and borrower funds, as long as the draw from HECM funds does not exceed the percentage approved by the Commissioner under the authority of § 206.25(a).

12. HUD Handbook 4235.1 Chapter 1-3(C). NON-RECOURSE

The HECM is a non-recourse loan. This means that the HECM borrower (or his or her estate) will never owe more than the loan balance or value of the property, whichever is less; and no assets other than the home must be used to repay the debt.

13. 24 CFR §206.27(b)(8). MORTGAGE PROVISIONS

The borrower shall have no personal liability for payment of the outstanding loan balance. The mortgagee shall enforce the debt only through sale of the property. The mortgagee shall not be permitted to obtain a deficiency judgment against the borrower if the mortgage is foreclosed.

14. HUD Handbook 4235.1 Chapter 1-13

A mortgage will become due and payable when the borrower dies, the property is no longer the borrower's principal residence, the borrower does not occupy the property for 12 consecutive months for health reasons, or the borrower violates the mortgage covenants.

15. 24 CFR §206.27(c)(1) MORTGAGE PROVISIONS

The mortgage shall state that the outstanding loan balance will be due and payable in full if a borrower dies and the property is not the principal residence of at least one surviving borrower, except that the due and payable status shall be deferred in accordance with paragraph (c)(3) of this section if the requirements of the Deferral Period are met; or if a borrower conveys all of his or her title in the property and no other borrower retains title to the property.

16. HUD.GOV – HECM Servicing
Frequently Asked Questions (FAQs)

HUD's regulations at 24 CFR 206.125(c) state, in part, that "[i]f the mortgage is due and payable at the time the contract for sale is executed, the borrower may sell the property for at least the lesser of the mortgage balance or five percent under the appraised value" (i.e., 95% of the appraised value of the mortgaged property). HUD interprets the word "sale" to include any post-death conveyance of the mortgage property (even by operation of law) to the borrower's estate or heirs (including a surviving spouse who is not obligated on the HECM note). A loan payoff that occurs simultaneously with or immediately following such a post-death conveyance will be regarded as a sale transaction for purposes of section 206.125(c).

17. HUD Handbook 4235.1 Chapter 1-4. PRINCIPAL LIMIT

The amount that the borrower can receive from a Reverse Mortgage is determined by calculating the principal limit. The figure increases monthly and represents the maximum payment that a borrower may receive. The principal limit at origination is based on the age of the youngest borrower, the expected average mortgage interest rate, and the maximum claim amount.

18. Mortgagee Letter 2020-42. Nationwide HECM Limits

For the period January 1, 2021 through December 31, 2021, the maximum claim amount for FHA-insured HECMs will be $822,375 (150 percent of Federal Home Loan Mortgage Corporation's (Freddie Mac) national conforming limit of $548,250).

19. HUD.GOV – HECM Servicing
Frequently Asked Questions (FAQs)

When a HECM loan becomes due and payable as a result of the mortgagor's death and the property is conveyed by will or operation of law to the mortgagor's estate or heirs (including a surviving spouse who is not obligated on the HECM note) that party (or parties if multiple heirs) may satisfy the HECM debt by paying the lesser of the mortgage balance or 95% of the current appraised value of the property.

20. 24 CFR §206.125(a)(2).
ACQUISITION AND SALE OF THE PROPERTY

After notifying and receiving approval of the Commissioner when needed, the mortgagee shall notify the borrower, Eligible Non-Borrowing Spouse, borrower's estate, and borrower's heir(s), as applicable, within 30 days of the later of notifying the Commissioner or receiving approval, if needed, that the mortgage is due and payable. The mortgagee shall give the applicable party 30 days from the date of notice to engage in the following actions:

(i) Pay the outstanding loan balance, including any accrued interest, MIP, and mortgagee advances in full;

(ii) Sell the property for an amount not to be less than the amount determined by the Commissioner through notice, which shall not exceed 95 percent of the appraised value as determined under §206.125(b), with the net proceeds of the sale to be applied towards the outstanding loan balance. Closing costs shall not exceed the greater of: 11 percent of the sales price; or a fixed dollar amount as determined by the Commissioner through Federal Register notice. For the purposes of this section, sell includes the transfer of title by operation of law;

(iii) Provide the mortgagee with a deed in lieu of foreclosure;

(iv) Correct the condition which resulted in the mortgage coming due and payable for reasons other than the death of the last surviving borrower;

(v) For an Eligible Non-Borrowing Spouse, correct the condition which resulted in an end to the Deferral Period in accordance with §206.57; or

(vi) Such other actions as permitted by the Commissioner through notice.

21. 24 CFR §206.205(a). PROPERTY CHARGES

(1) The borrower shall be responsible for the payment of the following property charges before or on the due date: ground rents, condominium fees, planned unit development fees, and homeowners' association fees.

(2) Payment of the following property charges are obligations of the borrower and shall be made through the LESA, by the borrower, or by the mortgagee, in accordance with paragraphs (b) through (e) of this section on or before the due date: property taxes, including any special assessments levied by local or State law, hazard insurance premiums, and applicable flood insurance premiums.

22. Mortgagee Letter 2014-21. CREDIT HISTORY ANALYSIS

Mortgagees must perform a credit history analysis, in accordance with FHA guidelines, for each prospective mortgagor to determine if the mortgagor has demonstrated the willingness to meet their financial obligations by analyzing each mortgagor's credit and property charge history.

23. Mortgagee Letter 2014-21. RESIDUAL INCOME ANALYSIS

Mortgagees must perform a cash flow/residual income analysis, in accordance with FHA guidelines, to determine the capacity of the mortgagor to meet his or her documented financial obligations with his or her documented income.

24. HECM Financial Assessment
and Property Charge Guide (Revised July 13, 2016)

Through the Fully Funded LESA the mortgagee will use HECM proceeds to pay property taxes and insurance premiums on behalf of the mortgagor. The mortgagor remains responsible for all other property charges.

25. HECM Financial Assessment
and Property Charge Guide (Revised July 13, 2016)

Through the Partially-Funded LESA the mortgagor will receive semi-annual payments from HECM proceeds to be used to pay property taxes and insurance premiums. The mortgagor remains responsible for timely payment of all property charges.

26. 24 CFR §206.17(b) ELIGIBLE MORTGAGES

A HECM shall provide for either fixed or adjustable interest rates in accordance with §206.21.

(1) Fixed interest rate mortgages shall use the Single Lump Sum payment option (§206.19(e)).

(2) Adjustable interest rate mortgages shall initially provide for the term (§206.19(a)), the tenure (§206.19(b)), the line of credit (§206.19(c)), or a modified term or modified tenure (§206.19(d)) payment option, subject to a later change in accordance with §206.26.

27. 24 CFR §206.21(b). ADJUSTABLE INTEREST RATE

An initial expected average mortgage interest rate, which defines the mortgagee's margin, is agreed upon by the borrower and mortgagee as of the date of loan closing, or as of the date of rate lock-in, if the expected average mortgage interest rate was locked in prior to closing. The interest rate shall be adjusted in one of two ways depending on the option selected by the borrower, in accordance with paragraphs (b)(1) and (b)(2) of this section. Whenever an interest rate is adjusted, the new interest rate applies to the entire loan balance.

28. 24 CFR §206.19(e). SINGLE LUMP SUM PAYMENT OPTION

Under the Single Lump Sum payment option, the Borrower's Advance will be made by the mortgagee to the borrower in an amount that does not exceed the payment amount permitted in §206.25. The Single Lump Sum payment option will be available only for fixed interest rate HECMs Set asides requiring disbursements after close may be offered in accordance with paragraphs (f)(1) through (3) of this section.

29. Mortgagee Letter 2007-13. THE LIBOR INDEX

In addition, this final rule amended HUD's regulation at 24 CFR 206.3 to add the use of both the 1-Month LIBOR index and the 1-Month Constant Maturity Treasury (CMT) index for calculating the interest rate adjustments on the monthly adjusting Home Equity Conversion Mortgage (HECM). The final rule also permits the 1-Year LIBOR index for calculating the interest rate adjustments on the annually adjusting HECM. The 10-Year LIBOR swap rate shall be used to calculate the Expected Interest Rate on LIBOR-indexed HECMs.

30. 24 CFR §206.21(b)(1). INTEREST RATE

For all annual adjustable interest rate HECMs, no single adjustment to the interest rate shall result in a change in either direction of more than two percentage points from the interest rate in effect for the period immediately preceding that adjustment. Index changes in excess of two percentage points may not be carried over for inclusion in an adjustment for a subsequent year. Adjustments in the effective rate of interest over the entire term of the mortgage may not result in a change in either direction of more than five percentage points from the initial contract interest rate.

31. 24 CFR §206.3 EXPECTED RATES

Expected average mortgage interest rate means the interest rate used to calculate the principal limit established at closing. For fixed interest rate HECMs, the expected average mortgage interest rate is the same as the fixed mortgage (Note) interest rate and is set simultaneously with the fixed interest rate. For adjustable interest rate HECMs, it is either the sum of the mortgagee's margin plus the weekly average yield for U.S. Treasury securities adjusted to a constant maturity of 10 years, or it is the sum of the mortgagee's margin plus the 10-year LIBOR swap rate, depending on which interest rate index is chosen by the borrower.

32. 24 CFR §206.3 DEFINITIONS

Mortgagees, with the agreement of the borrower, may simultaneously lock in the expected average mortgage interest rate and the mortgagee's margin prior to the date of loan closing or simultaneously establish the expected average mortgage interest rate and the mortgagee's margin on the date of loan closing.

33. 24 CFR §206.21(b) INTEREST RATE

An initial expected average mortgage interest rate, which defines the mortgagee's margin, is agreed upon by the borrower and mortgagee as of the date of loan closing, or as of the date of rate lock-in, if the expected average mortgage interest rate was locked in prior to closing.

34. 24 CFR §206.19. PAYMENT OPTIONS

(a) Term payment option. Under the term payment option, equal monthly payments are made by the mortgagee to the borrower for a fixed term of months chosen by the borrower in accordance with this section and §206.25(e), unless the mortgage is prepaid in full or becomes due and payable earlier under §206.27(c).

(b) Tenure payment option. Under the tenure payment option, equal monthly payments are made by the mortgagee to the borrower in accordance with this section and with §206.25(f), unless the mortgage is prepaid in full or becomes due and payable under §206.27(c).

(c) Line of credit payment option. Under the line of credit payment option, payments are made by the mortgagee to the borrower at times and in amounts determined by the borrower as long as the amounts do not exceed the payment amounts permitted by §206.25.

(d) Modified term or modified tenure payment option. Under the modified term or modified tenure payment options, equal monthly payments are made by the mortgagee and the mortgagee shall set aside a portion of the principal limit to be drawn down as a line of credit as long as the amounts do not exceed the payment amounts permitted by §206.25.

35. 24 CFR §206.31(a)(1). ALLOWABLE CHARGES AND FEES

Loan Origination Fee. Mortgagees may charge a loan origination fee and may use such fee to pay for services performed by a sponsored third-party originator. The loan origination fee limit shall be the greater of $2,500 or two percent of the maximum claim amount of $200,000, plus one percent of any portion of the maximum claim amount that is greater than $200,000.

36. Mortgagee Letter 2011-26 HECM COUNSELOR LIST

ML 2010-37 requires lenders to provide each client with a list of HECM counseling agencies. Effective with this mortgagee letter, the national and regional intermediaries that must always be included on the list provided to borrowers will include those Intermediaries awarded HECM counseling grant funds by HUD.

37. 24 CFR §206.41(a). COUNSELING

List provided. At the time of the initial contact with the prospective borrower, the mortgagee shall give the borrower a list of the names, addresses, and telephone numbers of HECM counselors and their employing agencies, which have been approved by the Commissioner, in accordance with subpart E of this part, as qualified and able to provide the information described in paragraph (b) of this section. The borrower, any Eligible or Ineligible Non-Borrowing Spouse, and any non-borrowing owner must receive counseling.

38. HUD Handbook 4235.1 Chapter 2-3(C). COUNSELING

The lender cannot begin the process of ordering a property appraisal or any other action that would result in a charge to the potential borrower until the borrower has received counseling, and the lender has received the counseling certificate from the borrower.

39. HUD 4235.1 Chapter 1-10 MORTGAGE INSURANCE

The borrower will be charged mortgage insurance premiums to reduce the risk of loss in the event that the outstanding balance, including accrued interest, MIP, and fees, exceeds the value of the property at the time that the mortgage is due and payable.

40. Mortgagee Letter 2017-12. Initial MIP Rates

The initial MIP rate is changed to two percent (2.00%) of the Maximum Claim Amount (MCA). The initial MIP rate is applicable to all borrowers and is no longer associated with disbursements made to or on behalf of the borrower at closing or during the First 12-Month Disbursement Period.

41. Mortgagee Letter 2017-12. Annual MIP Rates

The annual MIP rate is changed to one-half of one percent (0.50%) of the outstanding mortgage balance.

42. Mortgagee Letter 2014-07. NON -BORROWING SPOUSE

For any HECM with a case number issued after the effective date of this Mortgagee Letter, in order to be eligible for FHA insurance, the HECM must contain a provision deferring the due and payable status that occurs because of the death of the last surviving mortgagor, if a mortgagor was married at the time of closing and the Non-Borrowing Spouse was identified at the time of closing.

43. Mortgagee Letter 2015-02. REQUIRED DETERMINATION

At application, the mortgagee must identify any current Non-Borrowing Spouse and must determine if the Non-Borrowing Spouse is currently eligible or ineligible for a Deferral Period. This determination is a factual determination and cannot be changed or waived by any election. A Non-Borrowing Spouse that meets the Qualifying Attributes requirements at application for a Deferral Period is an Eligible Non-Borrowing Spouse and may not elect to be ineligible. Similarly, a Non-Borrowing Spouse that is ineligible at application because he or she does not satisfy the Qualifying Attributes requirements for a Deferral Period may not elect to be eligible.

44. HUD 4235.1 Chapter 1-5(C). LINE OF CREDIT

Under this payment plan, the borrower will receive the mortgage proceeds in unscheduled payments or in installments, at times and in amounts of the borrower's choosing, until the line of credit is exhausted.

45. 24 CFR §206.25(g). CALCULATION OF DISBURSEMENTS

The line of credit amount increases at the same rate as the total principal limit increases under §206.3.

46. HUD 4330.1 Chapter 13-21B.
ESTABLISH OR INCREASE A LINE OF CREDIT

A mortgagor may choose to make a partial prepayment to set up or to increase a line of credit without altering existing monthly payments. By reducing the outstanding balance, the mortgagor increases the net principal limit. All or part of the increase in the net principal limit may be set aside for a line of credit.

47. 24 CFR §206.27(b)(10). MAXIMUM MORTGAGE AMOUNT

If State law limits the first lien status of the mortgage as originally executed and recorded to a maximum amount of debt or a maximum number of years, the borrower shall agree to execute any additional documents required by the mortgagee and approved by the Commissioner to extend the first lien status to an additional amount of debt and an additional number of years and to cause any other liens to be removed or subordinated.

48. 24 CFR §206.47(a). PROPERTY STANDARDS; REPAIR WORK

Need for repairs. Properties must meet the applicable property requirements of the Commissioner in order to be eligible. Properties that do not meet the property requirements must be repaired in order to ensure that the repaired property will serve as adequate security for the insured mortgage.

49. 24 CFR §206.47(b). PROPERTY STANDARDS; REPAIR WORK

Assurance that repairs are made. The mortgage may be closed before the repair work is completed if the Secretary estimates that the cost of the remaining repair work will not exceed 15 percent of the maximum claim amount and the mortgage contains provisions approved by the Secretary concerning payment for the repairs.

50. NRMLA Ethics Advisory Opinion 2015-2

In addition to the requirement that the HECM Refinance have a case number assignment date that is at least eighteen (18) months after the closing date of the prior HECM loan being refinanced, for a HECM Refinance to provide the required bona fide advantage to a consumer, the HECM Refinance shall either:

(a) Be originated at the written request of the current HECM loan mortgagor to add as a mortgagor under the HECM Refinance a non-borrowing spouse or other member of the current mortgagor's family, who is residing in the principal residence of the current mortgagor and who is otherwise qualified to be a mortgagor; or

(b) Pass both a Closing Cost Test and a Loan Proceeds Test as each of those terms is further defined, below, in this Ethics Advisory Opinion 2015-2.

51. HUD 4330.1 Chapter 13-21B.
ESTABLISH OR INCREASE A LINE OF CREDIT

A mortgagor may choose to make a partial prepayment to set up or to increase a line of credit without altering existing monthly payments. By reducing the outstanding balance, the mortgagor increases the net principal limit. All or part of the increase in the net principal limit may be set aside for a line of credit.

52. HUD Handbook 4235.1 Chapter 1-2.
PURPOSE OF THE PROGRAM

The program insures what are commonly referred to as reverse mortgages, and is designed to enable elderly homeowners to convert the equity in their homes to monthly streams of income and/or lines of credit.

53. HUD Handbook 4235.1 Chapter 5-12.
PARTIAL PREPAYMENTS

A borrower may prepay all or part of the outstanding balance at any time without penalty. However, no prepayment of an amount in excess of the outstanding balance is allowed.

54. HUD Handbook 4235.1 Chapter 5-12(A).
PARTIAL PREPAYMENTS

Repayment in full will terminate the loan agreement.

55. HUD Handbook 4235.1 Chapter 5-12(C).
PARTIAL PREPAYMENTS

A borrower may choose to make a partial prepayment to set up or to increase a line of credit without altering existing monthly payments. By reducing the outstanding balance, the borrower increases the net principal limit. All or part of the increase in the net principal limit may be set aside for a line of credit.

56. Mortgagee Letter 2008-33. HECM FOR PURCHASE

The Housing and Economic Recovery Act of 2008 (HERA) provides HECM mortgagors with the opportunity to purchase a new principal residence with HECM loan proceeds. Section 2122(a)(9) of HERA amends section 255 of the National Housing Act to authorize the Department of Housing and Urban Development (HUD) to insure HECMs used for the purchase of a 1- to 4-family dwelling unit. Accordingly, eligible mortgagors now have the opportunity to purchase a principal residence with HECM loan proceeds. HECM for purchase transactions, for which the FHA case number is assigned on or after January 1, 2009, must satisfy existing program requirements and the provisions of this Mortgagee Letter.

57. Pfau, Wade D. 2015. "Incorporating Home Equity into a Retirement Income Strategy." Journal of Financial Planning

Meanwhile, opening the line of credit and that start of retirement and then delaying its use until the portfolio is depleted creates the most downside protection for the retirement income plan. This strategy allows the line of credit to grow longer, perhaps surpassing the home's value before it is used, providing a bigger base to continue retirement spending after the portfolio is depleted. Use of tenure payments or one of the coordinated spending strategies can also be justified as providing a middle ground which balances the upside potential of using home equity first and the downside protection of using home equity last. A key theme is that there is great value for clients to open a reverse mortgage line of credit at the earliest possible age.

58. 24 CFR §206.211(a).
DETERMINATION OF PRINCIPAL RESIDENCE

Annual certification. At least once during each calendar year, the mortgagee shall verify the contact information for the borrower(s) and determine whether or not the property is the principal residence of at least one borrower. The mortgagee shall require each borrower to make an annual certification of his or her contact information and principal residence.

59. HECM Model Adjustable Rate Note - Published 2/12/15.

All prepayments of the Principal Balance shall be applied by Lender as follows:

- First, to that portion of the Principal Balance representing aggregate payments for mortgage insurance premiums;

- Second, to that portion of the Principal Balance representing aggregate payments for servicing fees;

- Third, to that portion of the Principal Balance representing accrued interest due under the Note; and

- Fourth, to the remaining portion of the Principal Balance.

60. 24 CFR §206.107(a)(1).
MORTGAGEE ELECTION OF ASSIGNMENT

Under the assignment option, the mortgagee shall have the option of assigning the mortgage to the Commissioner if the outstanding loan balance is equal to or greater than 98 percent of the maximum claim amount, regardless of the deferral status, or the borrower has requested a payment which exceeds the difference between the maximum claim amount and the outstanding loan balance...

61. HUD 4330 CH13-29A

The mortgagor or the mortgagor's estate may sell the property at any time for the lesser of the debt due under the mortgage, or the appraised value at the time of the sale.

62. HUD 4330 CH13-29B

If the mortgage is due and payable at the time the contract for sale is executed, the mortgagor may sell the property for the lesser of 95% of the current appraised value or the outstanding balance.

63. FHA INFO #13-36

HUD interprets the word "sale" to include any post-death conveyance of the mortgage property (even by operation of law) to the borrower's estate or heirs.

64. 24 CFR §206.25(d). TIMING OF DISBURSEMENTS

Mortgage proceeds may not be disbursed until after the expiration of the 3-day rescission period under 12 CFR part 1026, if applicable.

65. Section 255 of the National Housing Act (12 U.S.C. 1715z–20). PROHIBITION AGAINST REQUIREMENTS TO PURCHASE ADDITIONAL PRODUCTS

The mortgagor or any other party shall not be required by the mortgagee or any other party to purchase an insurance, annuity, or other similar product as a requirement or condition of eligibility for insurance under subsection (c), except for title insurance, hazard, flood, or other peril insurance, or other such products that are customary and normal under subsection (c), as determined by the Secretary.

66. Mortgagee Letter 2018-06. Collateral Risk Assessment

For all HECMs, FHA will perform a collateral risk assessment of the appraisal submitted for use in the HECM origination. Based on the outcome of the assessment, FHA may require a second appraisal be obtained prior to approving the HECM.

Made in the USA
Las Vegas, NV
11 February 2021

17613157R00075